JAMES TENNEY BRAND
A Life in the Law: Country Lawyer, Oregon Supreme Court Justice,
Presiding Judge at Nuremberg War Crimes Trial of Nazi Judges
Paul J. DeMuniz

Published by Hellgate Press
(An imprint of L&R Publishing, LLC)
2305 Ashland St., #104-176
Ashland, OR 97520
email: sales@hellgatepress.com

Editor: Harley B. Patrick
Book design: Michael Campbell
Cover design: L. Redding

Cataloging In Publication Data is available
from the publisher upon request.

ISBN: 978-1-954163-86-7

JAMES TENNEY BRAND

A Life in the Law: Country Lawyer, Oregon Supreme Court Justice, Presiding Judge at Nuremberg War Crimes Trial of Nazi Judges

❧

Paul J. DeMuniz

To the past generation of men and women who sacrificed

so much to save the world from Nazi tyranny.

Contents

Introduction

During my tenure as chief justice of the Oregon Supreme Court, I
served on the board for the Conference of Chief Justices and chaired
the conference's education committee. In that capacity, I learned that
the Holocaust Memorial Museum in Washington, D.C. had a travel-
ing educational program called "Law, Justice, and the Holocaust: How
the Courts Failed Germany." I arranged for the museum to present
its program at one of our conference meetings. The program was so
thought-provoking and well-received that I later had it presented to
all of Oregon's state judges as well. It was through my interactions
with the Holocaust Museum that I first learned that Oregon Supreme
Court Justice James Tenney Brand had served on the Nuremberg war
crimes tribunal tasked with trying high-ranking judges and officials
of the German Ministry of Justice. At that time, I also learned that
playwright Abby Mann had consulted with Brand in writing Mann's
play *Judgment at Nuremberg*, making use of the personal files, transcripts
and correspondence that Brand had generated during his service in
Germany. Indeed, Justice Brand was thought to have been the inspira-
tion for Spencer Tracy's portrayal of Judge Dan Haywood in the 1961
movie version of the play.

Today, few Oregon lawyers and judges are familiar with Justice
Brand's life or his role at Nuremberg. From my perspective, however,
James Tenney Brand is an important figure in Oregon's judicial history,
and his life and legal career deserve to be fully and publicly docu-
mented. Fortunately, there is a wealth of information about Justice
Brand's involvement in the Nuremberg Trials that can be found in his
personal writings and documents. Those materials are publicly available
due to the generosity of Justice Brand's son, Thomas Bradstreet Brand,

who donated them to the Willamette University Mark O. Hatfield Library in 2001. In addition, other important materials exist that have been collected and preserved by Justice Brand's living grandchildren. My special thanks to them for generously allowing me the privilege of examining those documents in researching this book.

Justice Brand was profoundly affected by the acts that came to light in his Nuremberg courtroom. So much so that, in his personal copy of the published Nuremberg judgment he authored, he left a hand-written note: "The Nuremberg trials and the judgments thereunder will for centuries stand as bastions of human liberty and teach men in all ages they cannot violate the laws of God, justice, morality and decency and excuse their acts in the name of national expediency."

Unfortunately, subsequent generations have, to some degree, become calloused to the effects of fascism in general, and to the evil inflicted on the world by Nazi Germany in particular. I hope that this book will, in some small measure, reinvigorate in readers a healthy awareness of, and resistance to, totalitarianism in whatever future form it may take, while at the same time making the life of James Tenney Brand—small-town lawyer, Oregon Supreme Court justice, and presiding judge at Nuremberg—meaningful and inspirational to subsequent generations.

James Tenney Brand

Prologue:
Judgment at Nuremberg

In 1959 Abby Mann's play, *Judgment at Nuremberg*, was performed live on the CBS television program *Playhouse 90*. The play, a dramatic account of the United States' war crimes prosecution of German Ministry of Justice officials after World War II, was followed in 1961 by a movie of the same title produced by Stanley Kramer using a screenplay that was also written by Mann. The movie featured many popular movie stars of the day: Spencer Tracy starred in the pivotal role of Dan Haywood, a judge from the state of Maine appointed to preside over the Nuremberg trial panel, Richard Widmark portrayed a hard-charging Army prosecutor, and Maximilian Schell—whose performance won the Academy Award for Best Actor—played the German defense attorney representing the highest-ranking German judge on trial, a role filled by Burt Lancaster. Marlene Dietrich, Montgomery Clift, William Shatner (later of *Star Trek* fame), and Judy Garland all had supporting roles in the film, with both Clift and Garland receiving Academy Award nominations for their performances. Abby Mann won the Academy Award for Best Screenplay.

Although Spencer Tracy did not win an Oscar for his performance in *Judgment at Nuremberg*, movie critics nevertheless spoke highly of his role in the film. As one wrote in the trade publication *Variety*: "Tracy delivers a performance of great intelligence and intuition. He creates a gentle, but towering figure, compassionate but realistic, warm but objective."[2] What few knew at the time, however—and fewer realize today—was that Tracy's character in the movie was not drawn solely from screen writer Abby Mann's imagination. It was, instead, built upon the real-life judicial performance on the world stage in Nuremberg of James Tenney Brand, an Oregon lawyer and Oregon Supreme Court justice. This is his story.

CHAPTER ONE: A FAMOUS FATHER AND FAMILY ROOTS IN COLONIAL AMERICA

WHEN JAMES TENNEY BRAND entered the world on October 9, 1886, his father, Reverend James Brand, was 52 years old and the well-known Presbyterian pastor of First Church, a congregation integral to the religious identity of Oberlin, a small city in northern Ohio. First Church and the city had been joined at their beginnings. Oberlin was founded in 1833 by two Presbyterian ministers seeking to create a religious community that would closely adhere to biblical doctrine.[3] They named the community in honor of Johann Frederick Oberlin, an Alsatian minister who preached throughout the remote regions of France in the late seventeenth century. A year later they founded the Oberlin Collegiate Institute—eventually Oberlin College—with the intent of training missionaries to take God's word to the people of the American West, white and native alike.[4]

Although Justice James Brand's later success in the legal profession was likely derived from Brand's combination of keen intellect and hard work, it is also likely that his parents' intelligence, rectitude, and profound commitment to education provided a significant launching pad for their son. The Reverend James Brand was born in 1834 in a small log cabin in Three Rivers, Quebec, Canada. Although he could read and hungered for knowledge as a child, he received no formal education in Canada. Late in his teens, however, he made his way to Saco, Maine, where he lived with a sister while working as a carpenter. Eventually, the pastor of the church he attended told him that the congregation could provide some financial support for Brand's education so long as he was willing to enter the ministry. With that understanding in place, Brand entered Phillips Andover Academy while in his early 20s, where his advanced age made him a "man among boys." He graduated from Phillips Academy in June 1861.[5]

At age 27, Brand entered Yale College where he became the "patriarch of the class, its religious leader, and its poet." However, when the Civil War broke out Brand, having "grown up from childhood with [an] intense anti-slavery feeling," felt the need to "[contribute his] share to the cause of the country" and enlisted with the Connecticut Volunteers in 1862. In basic training in Arlington Heights, Virginia, he was appointed Color Sergeant of his regiment, requiring him to carry the regimental flag at the forefront during combat—an immediate target for the Confederate forces. During the first combat he saw at Fredericksburg, Brand "was wounded through the shoulder" early in the afternoon and lay on the battlefield between the two opposing forces until dark, when he managed to make it back to Union lines. Brand then spent six weeks in a hospital in Alexandria.

The elder Brand next fought at Chancellorsville and later at Gettysburg. Brand's regiment originally had 875 men. However, earlier battles had reduced the regiment to 75 men when the regiment's fighting began at Gettysburg. On the second day of fighting at Gettysburg, Brand's unit, the 27th Connecticut, reduced to 38 men "made a desperate charge down through the 'valley of [the shadow of] death' across the wheatfield." The ensuing battle that history would subsequently remember simply as "The Wheatfield" saw some of Gettysburg's bloodiest hand-to-hand fighting. As the battle roiled around him, Brand navigated a murderous crossfire to rescue his disabled regimental commander and carry him to safety; that act would later earn Brand a medal for heroism. In 1885, when survivors from The Wheatfield gathered there at Gettysburg to dedicate a monument to their fallen comrades; the Reverend James Brand gave the oration at the ceremony that followed.[6]

Gettysburg was Brand's last battle. He returned to Yale, graduated in 1866, and then spent another year at the Andover seminary preparing for the ministry.[7]

Juliet Hughes Tenney graduated in 1869 at age 20 from Abbot Academy, an institution also located in Andover, separated by a fence from institution that Brand had attended. It is likely that Juliet and James met while both were living in Andover and married sometime before 1873. The couple's first two children were girls, Mary, born in 1878, and Helen born in 1882.[8]

Rev. James Brand and Juliet Tenney Brand, father and mother of James Tenney Brand

By 1873 Reverend Brand had become pastor of the important and powerful First Church in Oberlin, where he served until 1899.[9] As pastor of First Church, the elder Brand was a prominent community figure, noted for his powerful oratory and his stance against the retail

sale of tobacco, alcohol, and the operation of billiard halls, positions
he advanced with determination as a leader in the Anti-Saloon and
Temperance movements of 1880s Oberlin.[10]

In 1884, Iowa College awarded Reverend Brand a Doctor of Divin-
ity Degree, after which he was referred to as Dr. Brand. In addition to
pastoring First Church for 26 years, Dr. Brand also wrote books and
papers that were distributed both locally and nationally, among them a
work entitled *The Beasts of Ephesus*, published in 1892. Dr. Brand's book
provided advice to young Christians on conquering the "the world, the
flesh and the devil," as Saint Paul described the spiritual opponents he
battled at Ephesus. That volume is still in print today.[11]

It is through his mother, Juliet, that Justice Brand's family roots
extended into the soil of colonial America. Brand's mother traced her
lineage to early Puritan leaders, including two Massachusetts Bay
Colony governors, Simon Bradstreet and Thomas Dudley, as well
as Anne Bradstreet, daughter to Thomas, and wife to Simon. Anne
Bradstreet married her husband when she was sixteen years old in
Northampton, England. Together with her husband and her parents,
she emigrated to America aboard the *Arbella*, as part of the Winthrop
fleet of Puritan migration in 1630. Anne Bradstreet would go on to
become recognized as America's first female poet, while both her father
and husband, in addition to serving terms as early colonial governors,
became founding fathers of Harvard College, with Thomas Dudley
serving as a signatory on the college's original charter.[12]

CHAPTER TWO: LIFE AND EDUCATION IN OBERLIN, OHIO

TRACING A FATHER'S INFLUENCE on a son is always a difficult proposition. That is particularly true in the case of James Tenney Brand. Brand's father died when the younger Brand was only 12 years old and little information exists today about his boyhood in Oberlin.

However, it seems reasonable to conclude, that his parents' high level of education, together with his father's unchallenged rectitude and over-arching prominence in the community, were significant in Brand's early years, factors that motivated him to excel as a student, and conduct his young life in accordance with the norms and values he had absorbed from his family. Brand excelled academically despite suffering from migraine headaches, which he believed were caused by the requirement that he write with his right hand in grade school, when he was definitely left-handed. By the time Brand had graduated high school he was a tall, slender young man with a lean, bespectacled face that reflected a powerful intellect.

Following high school, Brand entered Oberlin College and graduated with a B.A. degree in 1909. While at college, Brand was active in student affairs becoming class president, president of the student senate, and captain of the college's intercollegiate debate team.[13] Brand's participation on the debate team was consistent with his father's early efforts to educate himself, one of which was to join a local debating club while working as a carpenter in Maine.

Growing up, Brand suffered from a sinus condition so severe that doctors eventually advised him that he would enjoy better health in the western United States where the climate was different from that of northern Ohio. It is doubtful, however, that Brand's doctors would have considered the damp Oregon coast an ideal destination for a young man with severe sinus problems. Nevertheless, after his graduation from Oberlin, Brand ventured to Oregon, where he worked first on his brother Charles' apple orchard near Roseburg. Eventually, however, he joined the United States Forest Service and worked from 1909 to 1911 as a forest ranger on the southern Oregon coast near a town then known as Marshfield, renamed Coos Bay in 1941.[14]

In 1911, Brand was admitted to Harvard Law School and awarded several scholarships before graduating with a law degree in 1914.[15] Brand likely had little trouble in being accepted to Harvard's law program since he had been an excellent student in college and was, moreover, descended from two of Harvard's founders.

James Tenney Brand. Baby in mother's arms, circa 1888

Brand graduated from
Oberlin College in 1909.

The Harvard Law
graduate, 1914

Brand on horseback during his time with the
U.S. Forest Service, 1909–1911

CHAPTER THREE:
A LAWYER RETURNS TO OREGON

IN 1914, HARVARD LAW graduates would have had their pick of multiple high-powered and lucrative career opportunities in places like Washington, D.C., New York, or Boston. For his part, James Brand, chose a career path that did not appear to overtly capitalize on his Harvard pedigree. Decades later, however, Brand's Ivy League legal education would prove pivotal in his appointment to the Nuremberg military tribunal.

No record exists of the reasons Brand chose to return to the small coastal community of Marshfield, Oregon to begin his law practice. Perhaps Brand returned because he enjoyed his time there as a forest ranger, or perhaps he was simply comfortable with both the image of the small-town lawyer and the reality of a professional's life in a smaller community, or according to family lore, he returned to Marshfield because he thought it would become the next San Francisco. Whatever the reasons, Brand practiced law in Marshfield as a partner in the firm of Peck and Brand.[16] He became the Marshfield city attorney in 1916 and served in that capacity until 1927.[17]

In 1916, Brand married his childhood friend Irene Morley, a relationship that began when the pair were children in Rocky River, Ohio, where both families summered. Like her husband, Irene Brand was also a college graduate, with a teaching degree. The couple eventually had three children, a daughter Morley, born in 1917, and two sons, James, born in 1919, who died of spinal meningitis in 1929, and Thomas, born in 1926.[18]

During his 13 years of private law practice on the Oregon coast, Brand was both an active trial litigator and appellate advocate. As a lawyer in, and the attorney for, the town of Marshfield, Brand handled all manner of cases. The 17 appeals to the Oregon Supreme Court in which he is listed as counsel reveal that Brand's law practice encompassed municipal matters, personal injury, property damage, criminal law, business and corporate law, and forest practices.[19] Brand's record as an appellate lawyer was mixed, however, most of the cases he lost on appeal before the Oregon Supreme Court involved municipal matters that he had argued in his capacity as the Marshfield City Attorney.

In 1927, Brand was appointed by Republican Governor Isaac Patterson to the circuit court bench in Oregon's Second Judicial District comprising Coos, Curry, Douglas, Lincoln, Benton, and Lane counties.[20] Just as he had done as a lawyer, Brand handled all manner of cases as a trial judge and his deportment on the bench quickly earned the respect of the lawyers appearing before him, his fellow jurists throughout the state, and the public. Very few of the rulings he issued during his fourteen years as a circuit judge were reversed by the Oregon Supreme Court. Moreover, for several years during the depression of the 1930s, Brand voluntarily reduced his judicial salary by fifteen percent, an act that angered some of his judicial colleagues.[21]

From 1934 through 1935, Brand served as president of the Oregon State Bar Association. He was an active Bar president, at one point highlighting problems with Oregon's parole and probation system and advocating for change. In March 1935, he travelled to Seattle to address the Seattle Bar Association where he delivered a speech entitled "The New Deal and the Constitution."[22]

In 1937, Brand was a state leader in opposing President Roosevelt's proposal to change the number of sitting justices on the United States Supreme Court (Roosevelt's so-called court packing plan). In that capacity, he argued forcefully in various writings and speeches that Roosevelt's plan threatened the independence of the judiciary, as well as independent speech and thought.[23]

During his time in Marshfield, Brand was also active in the community, serving as a member of the local school board, president of the Marshfield Chamber of Commerce, and chairman of the Coos Bay Boy Scouts. Mrs. Brand was no less civically active in the Marshfield community, serving as a member of the Marshfield City Council, and the Coos County Public Welfare Commission.[24]

Brand with his son, Tom, circa 1926

CHAPTER FOUR: OREGON SUPREME COURT JUSTICE

THEN AS NOW IN Oregon, state Supreme Court justices were selected for six-year terms in state-wide elections. Should a justice leave the bench before completion of that term, the Oregon Constitution authorizes the governor to appoint a successor.[25] That successor, however, is required to stand for office in the next state-wide election. Until 1931, when judicial elections were changed by the legislature to non-partisan races, Oregon Supreme Court elections were partisan affairs identifying a judicial candidate as either a Republican or Democrat.[26]

While serving as a circuit judge in 1932, Brand ran for election to position two on the Oregon Supreme Court against sitting Justice Henry Bean. Justice Bean had been on the court since 1910 and, in the years that followed, had been re-elected multiple times as a "Republican" Oregon Supreme Court justice. The 1932 judicial elections, however, were Oregon's first nonpartisan contests for the judiciary. Brand's 1932 Voter Pamphlet followed the letter of the new law, making no mention of his political party affiliation, highlighting instead his education, intelligence, work ethic, and judicial record. Justice Bean, however, could not resist revealing his party affiliation in the Voter Pamphlet, stating that "[w]hile I am a Republican I have been endorsed by the voters of the Democratic party at three primary elections for justice of the Supreme Court, which is very gratifying."[27]

Brand lost his race against Justice Bean, however, Bean died in office on May 8, 1941. Three days later, *The Oregonian* newspaper published

An Oregon Jurist, Appraising "The Wave
Of the Future," Herewith Suggests . . . . *Oregonian Sun. May 11 - 1941*

An Answer to Anne Lindbergh

A Contributor Investigates the Logic of An Appealing Thesis That Has Engaged The Attention of Millions of Americans

JAMES T. BRAND is circuit judge, second judicial district at Marshfield, Or.

Mr. Brand took his law degree at Harvard, later became city attorney at Marshfield. He is a past president of the Oregon State Bar association and is a leader in efforts to improve judicial procedure in this state.

BY JAMES T. BRAND

ANNE LINDBERGH would have you believe that her "Wave of the Future," condensed in the Readers Digest, is a permanent wave. I would not.

Her essay is so full of faith and idealism, so subtly and appealingly written, that anyone who criticizes it must feel like a bad boy plucking the wings from a butterfly. One must regret to destroy the flowing magic of her theme by analysis and dissection, but after all, belief in magic is not at the moment the crying need of America.

"The old world we loved is going," she writes. . . . "Somehow the leaders of Germany, Italy and Russia have discovered how to use new social and economic forces . . . They have sensed the changes and they have exploited them. They have felt the wave of the future and they have leaped upon it."

AUTHORESS:
Sees Potential Good
In New Of . . .

ANNE LINDBERGH

JAMES T. BRAND

dites her morituri te salutamus of the American way of life.

Her idea of the new order which is to displace our "dying civilization" is either less definite or much less definitely expressed. Plainly she would have us swim with the wave of the future. But she has already got Hitler, Mussolini and Stalin astride that wave—the one they leaped upon. So at least we know the company we must keep as we ride.

Again and most definitely the new order is linked in her mind with the nazi discovery "how to use new social and economic forces" and how to exploit them. The death by assassination of European democracy attests the nazi discovery of the new force technique. So this at least is a part of Anne Lindbergh's dream "that is on its way in the gray dawn."

CLUE:
To Anne Lindbergh's Outlook Discerned

Now, before I analyze her argument, let me speculate for a moment about Anne Lindbergh herself. A psychiatrist would find in this charming authoress a study of profound interest. She recalls to my mind the theories expounded by Jerome Frank.

- The infant, says Frank, is born into a sense of effortless security, but as childhood passes he becomes aware of his inca-

Judge Brand's response to Anne Lindbergh's Reader's Digest
article appeared in The Oregonian *on May 11, 1941.*

an editorial by Judge Brand, entitled "An Answer to Anne Lindbergh" (Charles Lindbergh's wife). The editorial was a response to an article in *Readers Digest* authored by Lindbergh entitled "Wave of the Future." In her article, Lindbergh intimated that the fascist visions of Hitler and Mussolini were somehow better than the American way of life as it stood at the time. Justice Brand's rebuttal was widely acclaimed, distributed in pamphlet form, reprinted in newspapers across the nation, and inserted into the *Congressional Record*.

On May 14, 1941, Brand was appointed to the Oregon Supreme Court by Republican Governor Charles Sprague. *The Oregonian* newspaper article announcing Brand's appointment also noted the publication of Brand's rebuttal to Lindbergh, describing it as "one of the most devastating pieces of logic ever produced in this state, yet kindly." The newspaper concluded its praise of Brand, writing, "But his own people on the lower coast, or the profession of the northwest, will not be surprised. It was merely a foray into a lay subject for a jurist who, from the bench, has long been impressing all of those in contact with him. He is the right man, among all those available in Oregon, for the appointment to Justice Bean's place. We confidently expect him to make a truly brilliant record on the supreme court."[28] Brand was elected to a full six-year term in 1942.[29]

Oregon State Supreme Court, 1941.
Junior Justice Brand is on the far right.

From May 1941, until late 1946—when the Oregon Legislature granted Justice Brand a year-long leave of absence to participate in the Nuremberg tribunals—the State's Supreme Court issued opinions in approximately 87 cases. Of those 87 cases, the court wrote opinions in 10 criminal matters, eight of which were authored by Justice Brand. The cases involved a variety of malign acts, from murder and sexual assault to the theft of a calf. Together, they presented the court with a variety of procedural issues touching on the insanity defense, the correctness of jury instructions, and the admissibility of confessions. Justice Brand's opinions affirmed six convictions and reversed two. All of Justice Brand's opinions reflected a powerful analytical intellect, clear writing, exhaustive review of the trial court record, thorough vetting of a criminal defendant's legal arguments, and an overriding commitment to procedural fairness. However, that commitment to procedural fairness, by Brand and his Oregon Supreme Court colleagues, can be described as untethered to strictly defined constitutional/criminal procedure. More than two decades would elapse before the United States Supreme Court ruled in the 1960s that federal Bill of Rights protections—specifically the Fourth, Fifth, Sixth, and Eighth Amendments to the United States Constitution—applied to the states through the Fourteenth Amendment to the United States Constitution. For example, it was not until 1966, in *Miranda v. Arizona*, that the United States Supreme Court held that the Fifth and Sixth Amendments to the United States Constitution, applied to the states through the Fourteenth Amendment, prohibiting the prosecution from using a criminal defendant's in-custody statements unless a defendant had first been warned of the right to remain silent, the right to counsel during any interrogation, understood those constitutional rights, and had voluntarily waived them.[30]

Two of Justice Brand's pre-Nuremberg cases in particular—both involving the voluntariness of a defendant's confession—illustrate the court's, and Brand's apparent lack of a dogma regarding matters of criminal procedure. In *State v. Folkes*, the defendant Robert Folkes, a Black

JAMES T. BRAND
Coos man on state tribunal.

Brand Named To High Court

SALEM, May 14 (Special)— Governor Charles A. Sprague Wednesday announced the appointment of Circuit Judge James T. Brand, Marshfield, to succeed Justice Henry J. Bean of the state supreme court, who died here recently.

Brand is one of three judges serving the circuit court district embracing Benton, Coos, Curry, Douglas, Lane and Lincoln counties.

On May 13, 1941, Oregon's governor, Charles A. Sprague, appointed Brand to the Oregon state supreme court.

man, was convicted, and sentenced to death for murdering a woman in her train berth as the train passed through Linn County, Oregon on its way from Seattle to Los Angeles.[31] The defendant, a young dining room cook on the train, had allegedly made multiple confessions to authorities from both the Los Angeles police department and Oregon State Police. Justice Brand, writing for the majority conceded that a transcript of one of the defendant's confessions should not have been admitted into evidence. However, Brand and the other justices in the majority concluded that, in the light of the defendant's other confessions that had been properly admitted at trial, the erroneous admission of one such piece of evidence was insufficient to overturn the jury's guilty verdict and death sentence.

Justice Rossman, joined by Justice Kelly, authored a vigorous dissent, pointing out the lack of any physical evidence linking Folkes to the murder, and the unreliability of the alleged confessions due to questionable police conduct such as sleep deprivation and prolonged interrogation. In addition, the dissent noted, Folkes had denied his guilt in the statements he acknowledged having made, but police claimed that he had nevertheless confessed in two statements Folkes had neither reviewed nor signed. According to the dissenting justices, Folkes' so-called confessions had contradicted sworn testimony from police officers involved in the investigation and should not have been allowed into evidence.

Soon after the Oregon Supreme Court affirmed Folkes' conviction and death sentence, the Portland NAACP circulated Justice Rossman's dissent as part of a campaign asking Governor Earl Snell to commute Folkes' death sentence. Eventually, the campaign to save Folkes included a coalition of church members, clergymen, the Urban League, and railroad dining car workers' unions. The coalition asserted among other things, that Folkes' alleged confessions were involuntary, that there was a lack of any physical evidence connecting Folkes to the murder, and that there was another likely suspect—a white man—who, for overtly racial reasons, police had failed to meaningfully investigate. However, no assertion was ever made that the court's decision was tainted with racism. All of those extra-judicial efforts failed, and on January 5, 1945, Folkes was executed in the gas chamber at the Oregon State Penitentiary.[32]

Two years later, Justice Brand would reach a different conclusion regarding the voluntariness of a defendant's confession. In *State v. Linn*, the defendant had been convicted of engaging in a sexual act with a cognitively impaired minor, a conviction based primarily on the defendant's alleged confession.[33] Justice Brand, writing for a unanimous court, reversed the defendant's conviction, stating:

> This is not a case in which the guilt of the defendant was clearly and overwhelmingly established or in which there was competent and undisputed evidence of voluntary confessions other than that contained in Exhibit 2 [apparently a written confession]. Here the defendant had twice been tried, the first trial resulting in a hung jury. The prosecuting witness was a feeble-minded child and the evidence for the state was confused and in some respects contradictory. The confession was obviously the basis on which the verdict of guilty rested. Upon consideration of

the entire record and the undisputed evidence, we find that the defendant was influenced to execute Exhibit 2 by the deliberate employment of inducements and threats and that the receipt in evidence of that exhibit as a confession was error since it was not shown to have been voluntary. By its receipt, the defendant, whether in fact guilty or not, was deprived of a fair trial. His substantial rights were violated, and therefore the judgment of conviction must be reversed.[34]

Although both *Folkes* and *Linn* involved the admissibility of pre-trial statements made by a criminal defendant, the different conclusion in each case appeared to be based on Justice Brand's unblinking assessment concerning the overall strength of the evidence pertaining to each defendant's guilt. That trait would later enable Justice Brand to grapple fairly with the procedures arising under the international law of war that he would need to master and apply at Nuremberg.[35]

CHAPTER FIVE:
THE FIRST NUREMBERG TRIBUNAL

WHEN PRESIDENT FRANKLIN ROOSEVELT died in April 1945, the German Army was in its death throes and would surrender weeks later on May 8, 1945.[36] During the months leading up to Germany's surrender, there had been extensive discussion and debate among Allied leaders in the United States, Great Britain, the Soviet Union, and France about what should become of the Nazi leaders responsible for wartime atrocities considered to be some of the most horrendous experienced by human kind. The Allies had long been aware of the Nazi's murderous conduct, even before the United States entered the war. In early 1940, the United States Embassy in Berlin had transmitted news of the wholesale deportation of German Jews to Poland. Reports of Nazi territorial occupations in 1940 and 1941 described the roundup of millions of men and women from the occupied countries for forced labor in German mines and factories, while Soviet prisoners in German hands froze or starved to death. 1942 brought reports that Jews from the occupied countries were being exterminated in death camps as part of the Nazi's "final solution of the Jewish problem." By 1945, the names of many responsible for those atrocities were known to the Allies.[37]

Some of the Allied leadership, Russians in particular, but also Churchill and, for a time Roosevelt, favored a political solution for dealing with those responsible for Nazi atrocities—summary execution.[38] On April 14, 1945 United States Supreme Court Justice Robert Jackson spoke at Roosevelt's funeral, and later that same day gave a speech to the American Society of International Law in which he revealed his interest in prosecuting Nazi military and civilian leaders as war criminals. In that address, Jackson remarked that he was "not so troubled as some seem to be over problems of jurisdiction of war criminals or of finding existing and recognized law by which standards of guilt may be determined." Jackson nevertheless opined that "[y]ou must put no man on trial before anything that is called a court, if you are not prepared to establish his personal guilt."[39]

It may be that, in addition to Justice Jackson's reputation as a lawyer, and former Attorney General of the United States, President Truman had also become aware of Jackson's speech and was, to some degree, influenced by it. In any event, soon after Jackson's address, President Truman asked one of his top advisors, Judge Samuel Rosenman, to contact Jackson to determine whether Jackson would consider temporarily leaving the Court to lead a prosecution of Nazi war criminals. Jackson accepted Truman's offer on April 29, 1945, despite having little background in criminal law or procedure. Immediately, Jackson set about establishing the procedural and evidentiary rules necessary to govern the world's first international war crimes trial.[40] In doing so, Justice Jackson opined that "we must try to outline a flexible but efficient procedure that will be both summary and in keeping with our traditional fairness towards those accused of crime."[41]

However, getting the Allies to agree on the procedural and evidentiary rules for such post-war proceedings proved difficult. Meeting in London during the summer of 1945, Allied representatives vigorously argued over the procedures and form of a war crimes trial. In particular, the Russians aggressively opposed Jackson's proposed format modeled on the American adversarial trial system. That format required among other things, providing war crimes defendants with notice of charges, representation by counsel, cross examination of witnesses, and the right to testify. The Russians also opposed requiring that the criminal nature of the various Nazi organizations be proven at trial, along with the identity of accused individuals, and the personal guilt of each.[42] For their part, the Russians argued that: (1) the Allies should simply declare that Nazi organizations were criminal organizations; (2) the proceedings should focus only on whether an accused was a member of such an organization; and (3) once criminal responsibility for the leadership of those organizations was established, criminal responsibility for the organization's entire membership should be deemed automatically established as well.[43]

Finally, in August, the Russians tempered their objections with various concessions and the Allies reached an accord detailed in two documents called the London Agreement. Together, those documents reflected broad acceptance of Jackson's positions on procedure and evidence. The first document established that Nazi leaders would be prosecuted in an International Military Tribunal to be held at Nuremberg, Germany, the longstanding ceremonial touchstone of the Nazi party. The tribunal would begin in November 1945 and take place at the city's only-moderately damaged Palace of Justice.[44]

The second document—a charter—set out "the constitution, jurisdiction, and functions of the Tribunal." According to the charter, in tribunal proceedings accused individuals would have the right to: (1) receive a preliminary hearing; (2) have counsel, if desired; (3) present evidence; (4) cross-examine prosecution witnesses; and (5) receive a copy of the indictment specifying in detail the charges against them.[45]

Having decided to proceed with an international trial, the Allies also made explicit certain legal tenets that had only been implied before the war, namely that:

> to prepare, incite, or wage a war of aggression, or
> to conspire with others to do so, is a crime against
> international society, and that to prosecute, oppress, or do
> violence to individuals or minorities on political, racial,
> or religious grounds in connection with such a war, or to
> exterminate, enslave, or deport civilian populations, is an
> international crime, and that for the commission of such
> crimes individuals are responsible.[46]

Four judges, one each from Great Britain, France, the Soviet Union, and the United States, were charged with deciding the fate of twenty-four leading Nazis in the first war crimes trial held at Nuremberg. An affirmative vote by three of the four judges was necessary to find an accused guilty.[47] Francis Biddle, formerly a federal judge and Attorney General of the United States, was appointed by President Truman to serve as the American jurist. Consistent with the definitions set out by the allies in the London Charter, the defendants were indicted for "war" crimes, crimes against "peace," and crimes against humanity.

However, in addition, the indictment included a conspiracy charge, not explicitly defined in the London Charter. In that regard, the indictment alleged that the defendants acting pursuant to a common design, unlawfully, willfully, and knowingly did conspire and agree together, and with each other, and with diverse others present, to commit war crimes, and crimes against humanity.

The Nazi leaders named in the first tribunal "indictment" were Hermann Goering, Commander-in-Chief of the German Air Force and Chief of War Economy; Ernst Kaltenbrunner, Chief of Reich Main Security Office; Alfred Rosenberg, Minister of the Occupied Eastern Territories and Leader of the Foreign Policy Office; Hans Frank, Governor General of Occupied Poland; Wilhelm Frick, Minister of Interior; Julius Streicher, founder and publisher of the Anti-Semitic Newspaper, *Der Sturmer*; Arthur Seyss-Inquart, Commissioner of Occupied Dutch Territories; Martin Borman, Chief of the Nazi Party Chancellery (tried in absentia); Walther Funk, Minister of Economics; Fritz Sauckel, head of the forced labor program; Albert Speer, Director of the Armaments program; Rudolf Hess, deputy to Hitler for Nazi Party matters; Admiral Erich Raeder, Commander-in-Chief of the German Navy during the first half of the war; Joachim von Ribbentrop, Minister of Foreign Affairs; Admiral Karl Doenitz, who replaced Raeder as Chief of the German Navy, and for a brief period after Hitler committed suicide, was head of the German Government; Baldur von Schirach, National German Youth Leader; Konstantin von Neurath, Protector of Bohemia and Morovia; Hjalmar Schacht, Minister of Economics; Franz von Papen, Chancellor of Germany; Hans Fritzche, Minister of Popular Entertainment and Propaganda; Alfred Jodl, Chief of Operations of the Military Staff, who signed the instruments of surrender; Robert Ley, Chairman of the German Labor Front; and Gustav Krupp von Bohlen, Chairman of the industrial conglomerate that produced almost everything for the German war machine.[48][49]

Not named in the indictment, however, was Adolf Hitler, leader of the Third Reich, Heinrich Himmler, head of the Schutzstaffel (SS) and concentration camp programs, and Adolf Eichmann, the Nazi administrator who sent millions of European Jews to their demise in ghettos and death camps. Hitler was not indicted after his suicide in a Berlin bunker was confirmed. Himmler, likewise, escaped indictment and prosecution by killing himself while in British custody. Eichmann avoided prosecution by assuming a new identity and eventually making his way to Argentina.[50] He would later be captured by Israeli intelligence operatives in 1961 and executed after a trial in Israel in 1962.

The Allies' first war crime tribunal lasted 216 days, ending on October 1, 1946. Four thousand captured German documents were translated and entered as exhibits in trial, similarly, thousands of feet of captured German film, and a thousand still photographs were also entered as trial exhibits. Nineteen defendants were found guilty of one or more of the crimes charged against them and three were acquitted. Twelve of the convicted defendants were sentenced to death by hanging, three to life imprisonment, and four others given prison terms of 10 to 20 years. Among the Nazis sentenced to death and hanged were von Ribbentrop, Sauckel, Jodl, Frick, Streicher, Rosenberg, Keitel, Seyss-Inquart, and Kaltenbrunner.[51]

In December 1946, Justice Jackson submitted an aptly titled *Final Report* to President Truman detailing the results of the first war crimes trial. In that report, Jackson noted that the work of dispensing justice for German war crimes remained unfinished because many war crime participants remained unpunished. Jackson explained that their guilt "does not differ from those who have been convicted except that their parts were at lower levels and have been less conspicuous."[52] Nazis involved in the administration of German justice (e.g., judges, members of the Ministry of Justice, and prosecutors) fell within that category of so-called "lower level" offenders. As later categorized by Justice Brand, however, they were men, "who had fed innocent victims into the hungry maw of the terror courts of Germany."[53]

CHAPTER SIX:
A DECISION TO PROSECUTE
GERMAN JUDICIAL OFFICERS

WHILE THE FIRST TRIBUNAL was underway in late 1945, the four allied nations then occupying Germany adopted Allied Control Law Number 10. Under that law, each occupying country was authorized to establish a uniform basis for the prosecution of German war criminals and to establish tribunals within their respective occupation zones for the purpose of trying other Nazis, among them German diplomats, doctors, lawyers, businessmen, military leaders, and judges. Military zone commanders in each of the four zones were authorized to establish procedures for such trials to be conducted in their respective zones.[54] Importantly, Allied Control Law Number 10 also identified the actions that would be deemed criminal in those future war crimes prosecutions, drawing in the process, on well-recognized rules of international law that antedated the crimes that could be alleged in the indictments to follow.[55]

In Article 11 of Allied Control Law Number 10, the Allies defined the crimes that would be the basis for prosecuting "war criminals and other similar offenders, other than those dealt with by the [first] international Military Tribunal." Specifically, Article 11 section 1 defined the following acts as crimes:

> (a) **Crimes against Peace**. Initiation of invasions of other countries and wars of aggression in violation of international laws and treaties, including but not limited

to planning, preparation, initiation or waging a war of aggression, or a war in violation of international treaties; agreements or assurances, or participation in a common plan or conspiracy for the accomplishment of any of the foregoing;

(b) **War Crimes**. Atrocities or offenses against persons or property constituting violations of the laws or customs of war, including but not limited to, murder, ill treatment or deportation to slave labor or for any other purpose, of civilian population from occupied territory, murder or ill treatment of prisoners of war or persons on the seas, killing of hostages, plunder of public or private property, wanton destruction of cities, towns or villages, or devastation not justified by military necessity;

(c) **Crimes against Humanity**. Atrocities and offenses, including, but not limited to murder, extermination, enslavement, deportation, imprisonment, torture, rape, or other inhumane acts committed against any civilian population, or persecutions on political, racial or religious grounds whether or not in violation of the domestic laws of the country where perpetrated;

(d) **Membership** in groups or organizations declared criminal by the International Military Tribunal.

After defining the crimes that could be alleged against future defendants in Article II section I, section 2 went on to provide that:

Any person without regard to nationality or the capacity in which he acted, is deemed to have committed a crime as defined in paragraph I of this Article, if he was (a) a principal or (b) was an accessory to the commission of any such crime or ordered or abetted the same or (c) took a consenting part therein or (d) was connected with plans or enterprises involving its commission or (e) was a member of any organization or group connected with the commission of any such crime or (f) with reference to paragraph 1(a) if he held a high political, civil or military (including General Staff) position in Germany or in one of its Allies, co-belligerents or satellites, or held high position in financial, industrial, or economic life of any such country.[56]

By the end of 1946, the general scope of the trials to be held in the American Zone had been determined. There would be 12 separate tribunals involving charges of war crimes and crimes against humanity. Those charges would be brought against defendants such as the doctors who had performed medical experiments on prisoners; German industrialists who used slave labor during the war; high ranking German officers who had committed atrocities against prisoners of war; SS officers who perpetrated violence against concentration camp inmates; and finally, judges and other judicial administrators who had used the law to commit or facilitate the commission of war crimes and crimes against humanity.[57]

In accordance with Allied Control Law Number 10, American Zone commander General Lucius Clay promulgated Ordinance Number 7, setting out the governing procedures for future war crime trials to be held in the American Zone. Among other things, those procedures called for providing the defendants: (1) notice of pending charges by written indictment as well as pre-trial discovery of documents to be used at the trial; (2) a 30-day period between a defendant's arraignment on an indictment and the start of trial; (3) the right to be present at trial; (4) the right to be represented by counsel; (5) the right to present evidence; (6) the right to cross-examine witnesses; (7) the right to require prosecutors to produce witnesses and documents; (8) the admission at trial of *any* evidence having probative value (i.e. no application of American common law rules of evidence); and (9) the establishment of a defense information center to aid German defense lawyers representing the accused.[58]

With Justice Jackson's return to the United States Supreme Court, Army General Telford Taylor was selected to serve as Chief Counsel for War Crimes (chief prosecutor) for the remaining trials that would take place in the American Zone.[59] Taylor was a 1932 Harvard Law School graduate and following his law school graduation had worked in a series of federal government positions before World War II. During the war, Taylor, as a colonel, had served primarily in London, England as the intelligence officer leading an American group working with British intelligence at Bletchley

Brig. Gen. Telford Taylor

Park, analyzing German communications intercepted through ULTRA encryption. In the spring of 1945, as the war in Europe was ending, Taylor was recruited to serve on Justice Jackson's war crimes prosecution staff, serving as an assistant to Justice Jackson. In the first International Military Tribunal, Taylor led the prosecution team seeking to declare the General Staff of the German Army and the High Command of the German Armed Forces criminal organizations. That aspect of the war crimes prosecution failed.

General Taylor named Charles M. LaFollette as deputy counsel, Robert D. King and Alfred M. Wooleyhan as associate counsel, and Sadie B. Arbuthnot, as assistant to the prosecution team.

The military commander of each zone was authorized under the law to arrest any individuals identified as war criminals that remained in their zone. Eventually, 12 trials were scheduled for the American Zone—primarily Southern Germany—to take place again in Nuremberg.[60]

CHAPTER SEVEN: RECRUITING AMERICAN JUDGES TO JUDGE THE GERMAN JUDGES

UNDER ORDINANCE NUMBER 7, the United States War Department was charged with recruiting American judges from the ranks of "lawyers who have been admitted to practice, for at least five years, in the highest courts of the United States or… in the United States Supreme Court."[61] Because Chief Justice Fred Vinson, had been disturbed by the strain placed on other members of the United States Supreme Court by Justice Jackson's leave of absence, he invoked his supervisory power over the federal bench to forbid any federal judge from serving on the future Nuremberg tribunals.[62] As a result, the War Department was tasked with recruiting judges from state benches. Fourteen of the 29 adjudicators eventually appointed by President Truman were justices of their state's highest court.[63]

As part of the recruiting process, General Taylor expressed a preference to the War Department for the appointment of a judge from the western part of the United States, provided that the prospective appointee had been educated at an Ivy League law school.[64] Having discovered Justice Brand's Harvard Law background, War Department recruiters forwarded his credentials to General Clay, who then recommended that President Truman appoint Justice Brand as a judge on one of the future Nuremberg war crime tribunals.[65] Brand learned that General Clay's recommendation had been accepted when he answered a telephone call, and the voice on the line said, "this is Harry Truman."

WAR DEPARTMENT
WASHINGTON, D.C.

1 0   1947

Justice James Tenney Brand
315 North Summer Street
Salem, Oregon

Dear Justice Brand:

    I am pleased to forward to you a copy of the Executive Order
appointing you as a member of such Military Tribunals as shall be
formed for the trial of major war criminals.

    While in the European Theater of Operations serving in this
capacity, you will be subject to the orders of the Commanding General of the European Theater of Operations, as Military Governor
of the United States Zone of Occupation, for all matters not in
conflict with your judicial duties. For purposes other than that
of command, and without the responsibility of the comparable military grade, you will be entitled to the considerations and amenities
of a General Officer of the Army of the United States. The particular tribunal upon which you are to serve, and the specific position
thereon, will be determined by the Theater Commander.

    I wish to express my appreciation for your willingness to take
an active part in this important phase of our country's war crimes
program.

                        Sincerely yours,

Incl
As stated above   Secretary of War

FOR VICTORY
BUY
UNITED
STATES
WAR
BONDS
AND
STAMPS

*Letter confirming appointment of Justice Brand
to the Military Tribunal, March 10, 1947*

CHAPTER EIGHT:
THE BRANDS GO TO NUREMBERG

FOLLOWING PRESIDENT TRUMAN'S TELEPHONE call, the Oregon Legislature granted Justice Brand a one-year leave of absence from the Oregon Supreme Court and, in January 1947, Brand embarked for Germany. In Brand's own words, his "[t]welve hours on an Army plane marked the transition from a land where man had ranged the law against the criminal, to another land where the criminal had ranged the law against man."[66] Justice Brand was already in Germany when President Truman signed an Executive Order on February 27, 1947 appointing him to serve as a judge at Nuremberg.[67] After a contingent of tribunal appointees had been gathered together in Nuremberg, a supervisory committee was established tasked with assigning cases among the scheduled tribunals.[68]

American Zone commander General Lucius Clay eventually appointed Justice Brand to what became known as "The Justice Case." Justice Brand's colleagues for the Justice Case were Carrington Marshall, former chief justice of the Ohio Supreme Court and Judge Mallory B. Blair of the Texas Court of Criminal Appeals. Justin W. Harding, a former Alaskan judge, and an Assistant Attorney General in Ohio, was appointed as an alternate member of the tribunal. For purposes of the Justice Case, Marshall was initially designated the presiding judge, however, within a few months Marshall had to step down for health reasons, and Brand replaced Marshall as the tribunal's Presiding Judge.[69]

View of the Palace of Justice (left), where the International Military Tribunal trial was held. Nuremberg, Germany. November 17, 1945

View of Courtroom Two on opening day of the Justice Case. March 5, 1947

American judges appointed by President Truman to the Military Tribunal in 1947. Justice Brand is seated, center.

The Tribunal for Case Three in the series of OMGUS War Crimes Trials. Photo taken February 17, 1947, during the arraignment of fifteen former Nazi judges and public prosecutors. Left to right: Justice James T. Brand, Justice Carrington Marshall, Justice Mallory B. Blair, and Justice Justin W. Harding

In 1947, 39-year-old Hattie Bratzel was working by day in Salem, Oregon as a court reporter for the Marion County Circuit Court while attending law school at night in Portland. When it became public knowledge that Justice Brand was going to Nuremberg, Ms. Bratzel contacted the justice—whom she knew from his days as a trial judge—and inquired whether he would need a court reporter for the trials in Germany. Brand responded affirmatively, and soon Ms. Bratzel was also on her way to Nuremberg.[70]

Ultimately, Ms. Bratzel did not work as a court reporter on the Justice Case. She nevertheless proved invaluable to Justice Brand as his secretary and law clerk. Ms. Bratzel spoke fluent German, and each day throughout the tribunal proceedings she prepared written memoranda for Brand summarizing the relevant testimony and translating documents to be placed in files that Brand maintained on each of the defendants.[71]

In early February, 1947, Irene Brand boarded a ship bound for Bremerhaven, Germany. In an early letter home, Mrs. Brand described the ocean voyage as "calm" although she reported that she was seasick for 6 of the 10-day voyage across the Atlantic. From Bremerhaven, she boarded a train and was met by Justice Brand at a small train stop about 10 miles from Nuremberg. From there, they traveled to Nuremberg in a "beat up staff car with one star and GI driver, both assigned to [Jim] for his personal use."[72] The Brands were temporarily housed in Nuremberg's Grand Hotel while waiting for their assigned residence to be made ready. Irene Brand described their hotel accommodations as a "magnificent suite of three rooms with a bathroom as big as our dining room and a tub seven feet long."[73]

In letters home to their children in February and March of 1947, Irene Brand offered multiple observations about their life in Nuremberg. According to Mrs. Brand, ninety percent of Nuremberg was in ruins, there was nothing for sale, and no German shops were open. However, the city's Grand Hotel, Palace of Justice, and Opera House had been either partially or fully restored. Irene Brand estimated that at least 900 people were working on the Palace of Justice restoration to accommodate the 12 upcoming tribunal proceedings. Because Americans were prohibited from giving American money to anyone, the Brands had a food allowance, and had to charge their food purchases at an American military commissary. Cigarettes could be used for tips. Most American military uniforms did not display a rank insignia, only a United States patch.[74]

After a week in the Grand Hotel, the residence selected for the Brands, located in the Mogeldorf district of Nuremberg, was deemed ready for them to occupy. Mrs. Brand described the Mogeldorf area as a very old part of Nuremberg, with winding, narrow, cobbled streets, an ancient mill, a church, and two castles. On the properties where houses had been destroyed, shacks had been erected. The people living in those shacks had no water and no plumbing. Mrs. Brand was told that the "smells and dust from the walled city's remnants are terrific."[75]

Upon their arrival, the Brands were greeted at the gated entrance to the property by an armed Polish guard wearing a blue-dyed American military uniform. The house was only 10 minutes from the Palace of Justice. According to Mrs. Brand, their new residence was "camouflaged with bilious green paint. The house is ugly, no eaves, no porch—windows shuttered with green venetian blinds on the outside. The entrance hall is narrow, with side walls of brown and tan marble. The kitchen is in the front of the house. There's a large nicely furnished library and a huge living room, a [bigger] dining room and an open curved porch. Some of the furniture and pictures are beautiful, some cheap and ugly."[76]

"The house has been badly shot up with shrapnel [there were shrapnel holes in the French doors, over the door sills, and on the bathroom tiles], but not bombed." Sometime in early June, the Brands were contacted by Dr. and Mrs. Peter Stauerwald. Mrs. Stauerwald explained that she was the daughter of Nuremberg's former Burgermeister (mayor) who had lived in the house. Eventually, the Brands invited the couple to dine with them. During their dinner, the Brands learned that the couple had been "living in the house at the time of the [Allied] invasion, in their own air raid shelter when the bombing of the walled city took place." According to the couple, "18 SS men hid in the house and shot it out with the oncoming Americans."[77]

The Brand residence came with two German maids, both of whom had worked in a munitions factory during the war. One of the maids had not heard from her husband in two years and believed that he had either died in Russia or was a prisoner there.[78]

According to Irene Brand, "My life is simple—2 maids and a janitor relieve me of all duties except breathing." "We have no vacuum cleaner—the broom goes over everything every day, the scrubbing brush swishes all day long, the washing is done on a wooden cradle affair with a stiff brush." A maintenance man took care of the furnace and all the yards in the neighborhood. The Brands could have as many servants (paid for by the United States) as they wanted but were required to bear the cost of feeding them. Because Hattie Bratzel also lived with the Brands, the Brands were required to feed five on their two-person food ration.

Although Irene Brand recorded that Justice Brand worked day and night during the trial, there were opportunities for other activities. "We go to an opera or a concert two or three times a week," Mrs. Brand wrote. On one of their visits to the Opera House for a performance of *Carmen*, the Brands were seated in what had been Hitler's box.[79] The Brands also took time to visit other parts of Germany, as well as France, Luxemburg, Belgium, and to other European countries. In late February, just before the start of trial, the four judges selected for the Justice Case were summoned to Berlin by General Clay and American Ambassador Robert Murphy.[80] Together, the judges and their wives traveled to Berlin by private rail. According to Irene Brand, the train had a "kitchen, dining room, sitting room, two single staterooms, one double one, all in one self-propelled car. We had two engineers, a Staff Sgt., a cook, and a waiter to take care of us!"

Mrs. Brand described Berlin as a "wreck—entire downtown is ruined. The Brandenburg Arch stands, also the Victory Column; but the French have put their flag on top of the gilt figure. The Tiergarten is denuded of trees and metal statuary and Unter Linden has lost its Lindens. They have planted new little trees in the park[s]." While in Berlin, the couple also visited Hitler's Reich Chancellery, which she described as a "magnificent ruin, and went down into his air raid shelter where he is supposed to have killed himself and Eva. The shelter has many small rooms—all comforts of home—and two exits. The furnishings are all gone—were burned by the guards, to keep warm by. We were entertained in a palace—a guesthouse—and a club, where the plants were blooming orchids; dozens of small ones on a stem. The dining room was entirely in Chinese decoration—a dream room—but the china was Czech, chipped and battered, and the silver was all marked USN [apparently United States Navy]. The rugs were museum pieces." After walking around Berlin in a soft, quiet snow, Irene Brand commented that, "[t]he destruction is on such a large scale that it frightens you."[81]

CHAPTER NINE: SELECTING AND CHARGING GERMAN JUDICIAL OFFICIALS

AS CHIEF COUNSEL FOR War Crimes, General Taylor was tasked with determining which Germans should be charged with crimes in the subsequent tribunals, and preparing the written indictments that, when filed with the tribunal, would set forth the specific charges against the accused. The National Socialists' League of Law Guardians was a Nazi organization of jurists with about 100,000 members, any one of whom could have been charged with war crimes and crimes against humanity.[82] Taylor purportedly made his prosecution choices based on criteria consistent with the choices made for the first International Military Tribunal proceeding—i.e., responsibility for actions should be deemed greatest where authority was the greatest. However, many key leaders of the former German justice system were simply no longer alive. For example, Franz Gurtner, the first Minister of Justice under Hitler, had died of natural causes in 1941; Otto Thierack, Minister of Justice from 1942 to 1945 was captured by the British and committed suicide in British custody; Erwin Bumke, the chief justice of Germany (i.e., the presiding judge of the German supreme court) committed suicide in Leipzig in April 1945 as American forces entered the city; and Roland Freisler, Chief of the People's Court in Berlin, was killed in an American bombing raid.[83] Nevertheless, according to Taylor, "no one was indicted before the military tribunal unless in my judgment, there appeared to be substantial evidence of criminal conduct under accepted principles of international penal laws."[84] Eventually, for purposes of the Justice Case, Taylor charged 16 men who had held high ranking positions in the German justice system.[85] Those defendants were each listed in the indictment with a brief description of the position they had held in the German justice system:

Josef Altstötter, chief of the civil law and procedure division of the Ministry of Justice and *oberfuhrer* (senior leader) in the *Schutzstaffel* (SS), the black-uniformed elite corps and self-described paramilitary organization founded by Adolf Hitler in 1925.

Wilhelm von Ammon, counsellor for the Ministry of Justice's criminal legislation and administration division and coordinator of proceedings against foreigners for offenses against the Reich's occupational forces abroad.

Paul Barnickel, senior public prosecutor in the People's Court and a *sturmfuhrer* (lowest commissioned officer rank) in the *Sturmabteilung* (SA), the Nazi Party's original paramilitary wing.

Hermann Cuhorst, chief justice of the German Special Court in Stuttgart and member of the Nazi Party's Leadership Corps.

Karl Engert, chief of the Ministry of Justice's penal administration division and its secret prison inmate transfer program; an *Ortsgruppenleiter* (local leader) in the Nazi Party's Leadership Corps.

Guenther Joel, legal advisor and chief prosecutor for the Ministry of Justice; *obersturmbannfuhrer* (Senior Assault-unit Leader) in the SS and *untersturmbannfuhrer* (Junior Assault-unit Leader) in the *Sicherheitsdienst* (SD), the Nazi's first intelligence gathering and security service.

Herbert Klemm, state secretary and director of legal education and training for the Ministry of Justice, deputy director of the National Socialists League of Law

Guardians and *obergruppenfuhrer* (Senior Group Leader) in the SA.

Ernst Lautz, chief public prosecutor of the People's Court.

Wolfgang Mettgenberg, a high-ranking member of the Ministry of Justice's criminal legislation and administration division, and supervisor of criminal offenses against German forces in occupied territories.

Guenther Nebelung, chief justice for the fourth senate of the People's Court, *sturmfuhrer* in the SA and *ortsgruppenleiter* (Nazi Party political rank) in the Nazi Party's Leadership Corps.

Rudolf Oeschey, chief judge of the Special Court in Nuremberg, member of the Nazi Party's Leadership Corps, and executive of the National Socialists League of Law Guardians.

Hans Petersen, lay judge for the first senate of the People's Court and lieutenant general in the SA.

Oswald Rothaug, senior public prosecutor for the People's Court, formerly chief justice of the Special Court in Nuremberg, and a member of the Nazi's Leadership Corps.

Curt Rothenberger, president of the Court of Appeals in Hamburg, and Ministry of Justice state secretary.

Franz Schlegelberger, state secretary and later, acting minister, for the Ministry of Justice.

Carl Westphal, Ministry of Justice counsellor for criminal legislation and administration. Westphal was responsible for dealing with matters concerning criminal procedure and penal execution; he also coordinated nullity pleas against adjudicated sentences.

Of the 16 indicted defendants in the Justice Case, nine were officials in the Reich Ministry of Justice, while the others were members of the People's and Special Courts.[86]

In total, the indictment filed by General Taylor set out only four criminal counts. The first count, entitled *"The Common Design and Conspiracy"* contained seven paragraphs alleging that, between September 1933 and April 1945, all 16 defendants, acting as principals and accessories, took part in plans and enterprises involving the commission of War Crimes and Crimes Against Humanity, as set forth in Counts Two and Three of the indictment. Part of the defendants alleged common design and conspiracy had been to enact, issue, and enforce, certain statutes, decrees, and orders, which were criminal in nature, and to work with Nazi factions such as the Gestapo and SS for criminal purposes. In summary, the first count of the indictment alleged that the defendants had conspired to use the judicial process (1) as a weapon for the persecution and extermination of all those opposing the Nazi regime, regardless of nationality; (2) for the persecution and extermination of certain races; and (3) as a means—through the use of Hitler-appointed lawyers and laypersons—to turn the People's Court into a terror organization notorious for the severity of its punishments, the secrecy of its proceedings, and its general denial of judicial process to those appearing before it.[87]

All defendants were also charged with committing the crimes set out in Count Two. The second count alleged the commission of *"War Crimes,"* asserting that between September 1939 and April 1945, all the defendants had unlawfully, willfully, and knowingly committed War Crimes as defined in Control Council Law No. 10 against civilians in occupied territories and members of the Allied Forces who, during the war, had been captured and placed in the Reich's custody. In addition, Count Two alleged that, through use of the German courts the defendant's had created a reign of terror to suppress political opposition to the Nazi regime by subjecting civilians in occupied countries to criminal abuse of the judicial and penal process. Such abuses included repeated trials on the same charges, unwarranted imposition of the death penalty, pre-arrangement of sentences between judges and prosecutors, and discriminatory trial processes, resulting in murders, tortures, atrocities, and the plunder of private property.[88]

Although all 16 defendants were charged in Count Two, some of the allegations set out there linked specific defendants with specific acts. Paragraph 10 of Count Two, for example, specifically named defendants von Ammon, Engert, Klemm, Schlegelberger, Mettgenberg, Rothenberger, and Westphal, for crimes involving Special Courts that: subjected Jews of all nationalities to discriminatory penal laws and trial practices; denied them judicial process; and turned them over to the Gestapo either during or after service of their prison sentences for final detention in Auschwitz, Lublin, and other concentration camps.[89]

Paragraph 11 alleged, in turn, that defendants, Barnickel, Cuhorst, Klemm, Lautz, Mettgenberg, Nebelung, Oeschey, Petersen, Rothaug, Rothenberger, Schlegelberger, and Westphal had expanded and perverted German criminal laws to make petty misdemeanors and trivial private utterances treasonable for the purpose of exterminating Jews or other nationals of occupied countries. The result, the indictment charged, had been the murder, torture, unlawful imprisonment, and ill-treatment of thousands of persons.[90]

Paragraph 12 specifically charged that defendants, Klemm, Lautz, Mettengberg, Schlegelberger, and Westphal had, in connection with the unlawful annexation and occupation of Czechoslovakia, Poland, and France, integrated the German court system into these countries for the purpose of imposing sentences, including death, within hours of indicting individuals for crimes. Such actions, according to the Tribunal's indictment, had resulted—again—in the murder, ill-treatment, and unlawful imprisonment of thousands.[91]

In paragraph 13, defendants, Altstötter, von Ammon, Engert, Joel, Klemm, Mettgenberg, and Schlegelberger were specifically identified as having participated with the Gestapo in the execution of Hitler's so-called "Night and Fog" decree. Under that decree, civilians in German-occupied territories who had been accused of resistance against the occupying forces were spirited away for secret trial by Special

Courts in Germany. During such proceedings, facts surrounding the victims' whereabouts, trial, and ultimate dispositions were kept secret. In executing the Night and Fog decree, thousands of people were murdered, tortured, and illegally imprisoned.[92]

Paragraph 14 alleged that defendants, Engert, Joel, Klemm, Lautz, Mettgenberg, Rothenberger, and Westphal were responsible for, and participated in, the unlawful execution and murder of hundreds of non-German nationals imprisoned in penal institutions operated by the Reich Ministry of Justice.[93]

Paragraph 15 alleged that defendants, Lautz, Schlegelberger, and Westphal had, as Ministry of Justice officials, participated in the Nazi program of racial purity under which sterilization and castration laws were used for the extermination of Jews, "asocials," and certain nationals in occupied territories resulting in the murder and ill-treatment of thousands of people.[94]

Paragraph 16 charged defendants, von Ammon, Joel, Klemm, Rothenberger, and Schlegelberger with having unlawfully granted Nazi Party members immunity and amnesty in various court proceedings while discriminating against Jews, Poles, Gypsies, and other designated "asocials" by subjecting them to harsh penal measures and death sentences. Paragraph 16 also charged those named defendants with transferring all cases involving Jews to the Gestapo for "special treatment."[95]

Paragraph 17 alleged that defendants Altstötter and Schlegelberger had been responsible for decrees in which German citizenship for Jews in Bohemia and Moravia was forfeited upon their change of residence by deportation or otherwise. Following their loss of citizenship, the victims' properties were automatically confiscated by the Reich.[96]

Paragraph 18 alleged that defendants, Klemm and Lautz had actively participated in Hitler's program of inciting German civilians to murder Allied airmen forced down within the Reich.[97]

Count Three of the indictment was entitled *"Crimes Against Humanity."* Like the counts before it, Count Three also alleged that between

September 1939 and April 1945, all defendants did unlawfully, willfully, and knowingly, commit Crimes against Humanity as defined
by Control Council Law No. 10. According to that part of the indictment, the defendants had either ordered, abetted, consented to, or were
connected with, plans and enterprises involving the commission of
atrocities and offenses constituting, but not limited to, murder, extermination, enslavement, deportation, illegal imprisonment, torture, persecution on political, racial and religious grounds, and the inhumane
treatment of German civilians and nationals of occupied countries.[98]

Paragraph 21 of Count Three alleged that extraordinary irregu-
lar courts were used by all defendants in creating a reign of terror
to suppress political opposition to the German Reich. In doing so,
the indictment continued, German civilians and nationals of occupied
countries were subjected to criminal abuses of judicial and penal process
resulting in murder, brutality, cruelty, torture, atrocities, the plunder of
private property, and other inhumane acts.[99]

Paragraph 22 alleged that German Special Courts subjected certain
German civilians, and nationals of occupied countries, to discriminatory and special penal laws and trials that denied them any semblance
of judicial process. Those convicted in such proceedings were deemed
political prisoners and criminals, officially designated as "asocials," and
turned over to the *Reichssicherheitshauptamt* or Reich Security Main
Office (RSHA) for extermination in concentration camps.[100]

Paragraph 23 alleged that Germany's criminal laws had, through
various additions, expansions, and perversions perpetrated by the
defendants, become a powerful weapon for the subjugation of German
civilians and the citizens of other countries. The result, the indictment continued, was the systemic murder and extermination of certain
nationalities in occupied countries, as well as the murder, torture, illegal
imprisonment, and ill-treatment of thousands of Germans and others.[101]

Paragraph 24 alleged that defendants Klemm, Lautz, Mettgenberg,
Schlegelberger, and Westphal had, acting through various German

courts, aided and implemented the unlawful annexation and occupation of Czechoslovakia, Poland, and France.[102]

Paragraph 25 alleged that defendants Altstötter, von Ammon, Engert, Joel, Klemm, Mettgenberg, and Schlegelberger had participated in the Night and Fog decree whereby certain persons charged with offenses against the Reich or German forces in occupied territories were secretly taken by the Gestapo to Germany and handed over to the German Special Courts for trial and punishment.[103]

Paragraph 26 alleged that defendants Engert, Joel, Klemm, Lautz, Mettgenberg, Rothenberger, and Westphal, through their involvement with penal institutions operated by the Ministry of Justice, had subjected hundreds of German civilians and nationals of other countries to murder, brutality, cruelty, torture, atrocities, and other inhumane acts.[104]

Paragraph 27 alleged that defendants Lautz, Schlegelberger, and Westphal, acting through Special Health Courts in Germany, perverted eugenic laws and policies to the detriment of German civilians and nationals of other countries. Those actions, according to the indictment, resulted in the systemic murder and ill-treatment of thousands of persons, among them, German civilians and others who were committed to institutions for the insane and then systematically murdered.[105]

Paragraph 28 alleged that defendants von Ammon, Joel, Klemm, Rothenberger, and Schlegelberger had committed crimes against humanity based on the same facts underlying the War Crime allegations set out in Count Two, paragraph 16.[106]

Paragraph 29 alleged that defendants Altstötter and Schlegelberger had enforced discriminatory changes to German family and inheritance laws for the sole purpose of confiscating Jewish properties which, at the owners' deaths, were forfeited to the Reich.[107]

At the conclusion of Count Three, paragraph 30 of the indictment alleged that all defendants had committed crimes against humanity by suspending or quashing criminal processes and inciting German civilians to murder Allied airmen forced down within the Reich.[108]

The indictment's final set of charges—set out as Count Four—was entitled *"Membership in Criminal Organizations."* Paragraphs 32, 33, and 34 alleged that defendants Altstötter, Cuhorst, Engert, and Joel were guilty of membership in the SS, that defendants Cuhorst, Oeschey, Nebelung, and Rothaug were guilty of membership in the Nazi Party's Leadership Corps, and that defendant Joel was guilty of membership in the SD. All of the organizations noted in Count Four had been declared to be criminal enterprises by the International Military Tribunal in Case No. 1.[109]

CHAPTER TEN:
THE GERMAN DEFENSE LAWYERS

BEFORE TRIAL, ALL DEFENDANTS were informed of their right to be represented by counsel of their own choosing. Eventually, each had lawyers either qualified to conduct cases in German courts or approved by the Tribunal. Many of the German lawyers had themselves been members of the Nazi party and could have been subject to arrest and prosecution in denazification proceedings.[110] However, sometime before the first prosecution of the most senior Nazi war criminals, American authorities had arranged immunity agreements for many German lawyers to ensure that defendants in tribunal proceedings could be represented by counsel of their choice.[111]

All German defense lawyers received a daily food ration allowance of 3900 calories, three times that allotted to the average German. The defense lawyers also received one carton of American cigarettes per week, office space, clerical help, and a salary of 3500 marks per defendant. Benjamin B. Ferencz, chief prosecutor in Tribunal case Number Nine (the *Einsatzgruppen* case), alluded to the substantial resources provided to the German defense lawyers by noting that "the assistance given the [Nuremberg] defendants for the preparation and presentation of their defense [was] greater than that available to the average impecunious defendant in America."[112]

Two of the defense lawyers in the Justice Case, Egon Kubuschok—representing Wilhelm von Ammon and Franz Schlegelberger—and Hanns Marx, a former Nazi Storm Trooper who represented Karl Engert, had also been defense counsel in the first Nazi war crimes tribunal. During that first proceeding, Kubuschok had defended Franz von Papen, a former Reich Chancellor, and gained von Papen's acquittal. Hanns Marx, however, had not been as successful in his defense of Julius Streicher, founder and publisher of the antisemitic newspaper *Der Sturmer*. Streicher was ultimately convicted of crimes against humanity in the first tribunal proceeding, sentenced to death, and hanged.

Looking towards the defendants' dock in Court Two on opening day

The Justice Case tribunal would eventually declare a mistrial regarding Marx's client, Engert, but Marx himself nevertheless managed to create trouble for himself with the tribunal. At some point during trial, Marx had apparently tried to mislead the tribunal by "substitut[ing] a portion of a document pertaining to Engert's physical condition." When Marx's conduct was discovered, Brand found him guilty of "mutilating evidence and contempt of court," summarily sentencing Marx to 30 days in jail. According to Brand, "[Marx had] never heard of contempt of court and was very much surprised and put out about it."[113] Some of the defense lawyers in the Justice Case would go on to represent other defendants in subsequent tribunal proceedings.

CHAPTER ELEVEN: TRIBUNAL NUMBER THREE— THE JUSTICE CASE TRIAL

OFFICIAL PROCEEDINGS IN THE Justice Case began with the defendants' arraignment on February 17, 1947. In those proceedings, counsel for each of the defendants was present, the charges against each defendant were read aloud with simultaneous German interpretation, and each defendant entered a plea of not guilty. The tribunal then recessed until March 5th for the primary purpose of allowing defense counsel to continue their trial preparation.[114]

Some years after his experience at Nuremberg, Justice Brand reflected on an incident that occurred during that arraignment. According to Brand, as the charges were being read, "two of the defendants, in great agitation, interrupted the proceedings to insist that they be given some opportunity to defend themselves before being sentenced." The defendants in question were among those who, after routinely conducting sham trials, either imposed immediate death sentences on thousands of defendants or turned them over to the Gestapo for extra-judicial execution or death in the concentration camps. Justice Brand noted that the two German defendants had thought that their own system of Nazi justice was to be applied to them as well.[115]

Irene Brand attended nearly every day of the proceedings and recorded many of her observations, thoughts, and opinions in letters home to family. Getting her first look at the defendants, she noted that they "looked surprisingly like down-at-the-heels gentlemen. Not a bestial face in the outfit as far as I could see."[116]

*General Telford Taylor delivers the opening
statement in the Justice Case.*

General Taylor addresses the tribunal.

On March 5, 1947, General Taylor stood at the podium in Nuremberg's Palace of Justice and delivered the prosecution's opening statement. Before trial had begun, Taylor's written opening statement had been translated into German and provided to the defendants and their lawyers. In the first two sentences of his opening statement, Taylor framed the uniqueness of the case before the tribunal: "This case is unusual, in that these defendants are charged with crimes committed in the name of the law. These men, together with their deceased or fugitive colleagues, were the embodiment of what passed for justice in the Third Reich."[117]

Taylor went on to describe the law as practiced under the Third Reich and explained, using charts, the German judicial system and its hierarchy, as well as the leadership position that each of the defendants held in that system. According to Taylor, "the root of the accusation here is that these men, leaders in the German judicial system, consciously and deliberately suppressed the law, engaged in an unholy masquerade of brutal tyranny disguised as justice, and converted the German judicial system to an engine of despotism, conquest, pillage, and slaughter." Taylor characterized the extensive charges set out in the indictment as describing: "judicial murder and other atrocities, which [the defendants] committed by destroying law and justice in Germany, and then utilizing the emptied forms of legal process for persecution, enslavement and extermination on a large scale."[118] According to Taylor:

> Two facts stand out when we study the crimes charged
> in this indictment. First, the diabolical novelty presented
> by the designed use of a nation's system of Justice and
> its machinery by the governing power of that nation,
> as a weapon of destruction—an instrumentality of
> murder, kidnapping, slavery, torture, brutality and
> larceny. Second, the mass character and therefore the
> enormity of the crimes committed by these defendants
> with this new weapon—this headman's axe fashioned
> from the scales of justice in a forge, stoked with national

greed and racial bigotry and hatred, fanned by blasts
of directed propaganda and shaped by the calculated
blows of designedly infamous legislation, controlled and
dominated courts, and studied effort to make ineffective
or to eliminate completely, the defensive aids customarily
enjoyed by defendants in the courts of civilized nations.[119]

Following Taylor's lengthy opening, the prosecution informed the
tribunal that the majority of its evidence would be documentary. Deputy
Chief Prosecutor Charles LaFollette then described the process of
assembling that evidence:

As the Army overran German occupied territory and then
Germany itself, certain specialized personnel seized enemy
documents, records and archives. Such documents were
assembled in temporary centers. Later fixed document
centers were established in Germany and Austria where
these documents were assembled and the slow process
of indexing and cataloguing was begun. In preparing
for trials subsequent to the IMT (International Military
Tribunal) personnel thoroughly conversant with the
German language were given the task of searching for
and selecting captured enemy documents which disclosed
information relating to the prosecution of Axis war
criminals. Lawyers and Research Analysts were placed
on duty at various document centers and also dispatched
on individual missions to obtain original documents or
certified photostats thereof. The documents were screened
by German speaking analysts to determine whether
or not they might be valuable as evidence. Photostatic
copies were then made of the original documents and the
original documents returned to the files in the document
centers. These photostatic copies were certified by the
analysts to be true and correct copies of the original
documents. German speaking analysts, either at the

document center or in [Nuremberg], then prepared a summary of the document with appropriate references to personalities involved, index headings, information as to the source of the document, and the importance of the documents to a particular division of OCC.[120]

From those seized papers and records, "document books" were prepared containing an extensive biographical affidavit on each defendant, written copies of speeches given by a defendant, including speeches delivered to the defendants by Hitler, Goebbels and other leading Nazis, written copies of judicial orders signed by the defendants, and other documents revealing each defendants' participation and leadership in the commission of the crimes alleged against them.

On March 16, following the initial introduction of three such "document books" into evidence, the prosecution called its first witness, Konrad Ferdinand Wilhelm Behl. Behl was a German judge thrown out of office by the Nazi Party in 1935. According to Behl, "when German judges were ordered to wear the Nazi insignia on their robes everybody understood that this was the visible sign of the end of their [judicial] independence." Under questioning, Behl rebutted much of the defendants' claimed ignorance regarding German atrocities, and the Nazi policies of enslavement, and extermination. According to Behl, everyone who worked in the Ministry of Justice was "fully informed" about the activities of the Gestapo, the security police, and SS and "without any doubt knew what was happening in the concentration camps."[121]

While attending nearly every day of the trial, Irene Brand recorded her own observations concerning those proceedings in letters home. Among other things, she noted the compelling nature of the prosecution's witnesses. Mrs. Brand was especially impressed with the demeanor and testimony of a German woman who had been imprisoned by the Nazis because she had expressed her opinion during a tea that Germany was losing the war. She was subsequently taken into custody without an arraignment on any criminal charge and then released seven months later without any further explanation. According to Irene Brand, the witness seemed to know the defendants and had a subtle way of insulting them from the witness stand.[122]

Konrad Ferdinand Wilhelm Behl was the first witness to appear before the court. A former German judge, he was thrown out of office by the Nazi Party in 1935.

During trial, captured German movie footage of various Nazi atrocities, profoundly affected Mrs. Brand. After viewing the films, she opined that the defendants "ought to be shot—after a fair trial of course." Her contempt for the Germans was also fueled by an Easter weekend trip to Prague, Czechoslovakia. While there, the Brands drove out of the city to what had once been the village of Lidice. Irene Brand described the scene this way:

There is no sign that the village which housed 300 people was ever there. Literally, not one stone was left upon another. A crude wooden cross with a circle of barbed wire marks the spot where the men (178) were shot. A granite slab tells that here the 'Nazi barbarians' shot the men and scattered the women and children. Signs mark in three languages the sites of the mill, the church, and the school. They even smashed the gravestones in the cemetery. I felt like choking every German I met.[123]

For more than three months, the prosecution relentlessly assailed the German judicial system under the defendants' leadership, introducing evidence establishing that the system they led had functioned as an instrumentality of murder, kidnapping, slavery, torture, brutality and larceny. In doing so, the prosecution introduced 641 documentary exhibits—much of which consisted of the defendants' own judicial documents—documents that the defendants had no grounds to challenge based on authenticity—and presented oral testimony from 138 witnesses.[124]

Evidence introduced against two of the Justice Case defendants—Franz Schlegelberger and Oswald Rothaug—illustrates how the prosecution established individual culpability for each of the crimes charged in the indictment. In Schlegelberger's case, Jewish merchant Markus Luftglass had been charged and convicted in a German Special Court of stealing and hoarding a large number of eggs. He was subsequently sentenced to two-and-a-half years in prison for the theft. Hitler, however, apparently read about the sentence in a newspaper and informed Schlegelberger, then a leading official in the Ministry of Justice, that the punishment was unacceptably lenient and must be increased. Within a week, Schlegelberger had Luftglass turned over to the Gestapo where he was summarily executed. A captured German document revealed that Schlegelberger had written the following to Hitler regarding the Luftglass case: "My Fuehrer, the Jew has been turned over to the Gestapo for execution."[125]

Regarding Rothaug, the prosecution introduced evidence identifying Rothaug's perversion of justice in a case involving an elderly Jewish man, Leo Katzenberger. Katzenberger had been charged with "race defilement" for allegedly having sexual relations with a young woman named Irene Seiler in violation of the Law for the Protection of German Blood and German Honor. The trial took place in 1942 and, just before the charges were to be dismissed for lack of evidence (Seiler had steadfastly maintained that their relationship was only platonic), Rothaug intervened in the case and worked closely with the prosecutor to find a theory upon which Katzenberger could be found guilty. Irene Seiler later testified before the Justice Case tribunal that Katzenberger was a family friend who had owned the building in Nuremberg where she ran a "photographic store." Seiler indicated that in 1941, she had been arrested on suspicion of perjury, apparently because she had maintained that her relationship with Katzenberger was platonic. She described the Katzenberger trial in 1942 as lasting two days throughout which Rothaug, as presiding judge, had made various disparaging comments about Jews. Seiler remembered Rothaug's comments being directed to the courtroom audience and particularly recalled Rothaug's observation that she and Katzenberger were "liars," and that "racial defilement" through sexual intercourse between Jews and Aryans would "pollute the blood of generations."[126]

Ultimately, Rothaug prevented Seiler and Katzenberger from testifying that they had not had a sexual relationship. Rothaug found Katzenberger guilty by combining the Law for the Protection of German Blood and Honor, with a violation of the Ordinance Against Public Enemies. The latter edict authorized judges to increase criminal penalties up to and including death, in cases where a judge determined that a defendant had used the conditions of war to further their crimes. Katzenberger, was found guilty without any evidence supporting the charges against him and was subsequently beheaded.[127]

The Justice Case defendants did not proffer an opening statement of their own until the prosecution had completed presenting its evidence.

Each defendant was represented by a German lawyer, and each lawyer would go on to give a detailed opening statement attempting to rebut the evidence introduced against their client. However, the German defense lawyers had apparently elected Egon Kubuschok—counsel for Schlegelberg and von Ammon—to present a general statement to the tribunal outlining common defense claims applicable to all defendants.

On June 23rd—the day scheduled for Kubuschok to present his opening statement—Justice Brand announced that presiding Judge Marshall had been forced to resign his post due to illness and that Brand had been named the new presiding member of the tribunal. According to Irene Brand, her husband was relieved that Marshall had resigned. "[James] is dying to write the opinion. Blair and Harding are good men and pleasant to work with."[128]

Justice Brand listening to German defense counsel's statement, circa June 1947

After Brand's announcement, Kubuschok, in a statement alternating historic and academic antecedents, set about to rebut the prosecution's claims. Regarding many of the German judicial orders and documents introduced by the prosecution, Kubuschok contended that a defendant's signature on a sentencing order, in many instances, reflected only the defendant's official notice of the matter, not an acknowledgment of responsibility for the sanctions and outcomes recorded in the document. Kubuschok also asserted that the German judiciary had, for the most part, found Hitler, Himmler, and Bormann to be repugnant, a fact, Kubuschok argued, that had placed the judiciary "in a spot similar to that of an isolated animal at bay." According to Kubuschok, the German judiciary had been under constant assault by the Nazi party relentlessly advancing its own interests in opposition to that of the judiciary's, a fact that had supposedly weakened judicial institutions. Kubuschok pointed out that Himmler, for example, had attempted—albeit unsuccessfully— to wrest all public prosecutors away from judicial administration and absorb them into the mechanism of his Nazi police.[129]

Focusing next on the prosecution's claims that the defendants had subverted and misapplied substantive law, Kubuschok asserted that: (1) the defendants had never applied any law *ex post facto*;[130] (2) the judiciary's participation in Hitler's Night and Fog directive was justified as a military necessity and that the defendants had, in any event, imposed only a small "quota of death sentences" in those cases; (3) the defendants had neither created nor enacted the sterilization and euthanasia laws; (4) the defendants had never applied the sterilization law for political or race-related purposes; and (5) the defendants had actually thwarted enforcement of Hitler's euthanasia law, leading eventually to the program's demise.[131]

On June 25, 1947, defendants began presenting their respective cases. The defendants presented testimony from 47 defense witnesses, introduced hundreds of affidavits, 1,452 documentary exhibits, and 13 of the defendants testified on their own behalf. Defendant Klemm's testimony was typical of the defense proffered by those defendants. According to Klemm, he had never been political; he had thought a strong government would strengthen the German judiciary, but had never thought

Hitler intended to go to war. Klemm also claimed that he knew nothing about any of the documents on which his initials appeared, had never listened to a foreign radio broadcast, had never interacted with the Gestapo, and was unaware that "race defilers" who completed their prison sentences, were then turned over to the Gestapo for transportation to concentration camps.[132]

The introduction of evidence and closing arguments in the Justice Case concluded on October 18, 1947.

CHAPTER TWELVE:
JUDGMENT AT NUREMBERG

BETWEEN OCTOBER 18TH AND December 2nd, the tribunal studied the evidence before it. During that time, Brand began drafting the tribunal's detailed and extensive judgment. Undoubtedly, the daily summaries of documents and testimony prepared for him by Hattie Bratzel were of immense help in that process. The resulting judgment document was translated into German and provided to the defense lawyers and their clients before the tribunal reconvened on December 3rd. For the next two days, the tribunal judges took turns reading from the judgment authored primarily by James Brand.[133]

At the outset, the tribunal asserted that despite the defendants' testimony proclaiming their ignorance of the Nazi atrocities detailed in the courtroom for nearly a year, the defendants' own documents such as their judicial orders and decrees proved their criminality: "In rendering this judgment it should be said that the case against the defendants is chiefly based upon captured German documents, the authenticity of which is unchallenged."[134]

Next, Justice Brand, writing for the tribunal, addressed the question—by what authority was the tribunal empowered to try and order the punishment of the defendants named in the indictment? Brand addressed that issue at some length in the written judgment. In summary, however, Brand established the tribunal's jurisdiction and power based on the following facts and legal premises: (1) Germany's surrender on May 8, 1945 was preceded by the complete disintegration of the central government followed by the complete Allied occupation of all of Germany; (2) there were no opposing German forces in the field and the officials who during the war had exercised the powers of the Reich government were either dead, in prison or in hiding; (3) on June 5, 1945 the Allied Powers announced that they had assumed supreme authority over Germany, including all the powers possessed by the German government; and (4) the circumstances of Germany's unconditional surrender resulted in the transfer of sovereignty to the Allies. Based on the foregoing, the Allied powers were not a belligerent occupying force, and therefore not subject to the limitations set forth in the rules of land warfare. Accordingly, the Allies had the legal right to enact Allied Control Law 10, defining crimes against humanity, and establishing the Nuremberg tribunals for the prosecution and punishment of those persons who, prior to the Allied occupation, were guilty of committing those crimes. Brand added, that although Allied Control Law 10 on its face was limited to the punishment of German nationals, that did not transform the tribunal into a German court. Rather, the tribunal drew its sole power and jurisdiction from the will and command of the four occupying powers.[135]

Earlier in the Justice Case proceedings, defense lawyers had challenged the jurisdiction of the tribunal to decide whether the defendants were guilty of conspiracy as a separate substantive crime under Count One of the indictment. Justice Brand, the first to read from the written judgment, stated that the tribunal agreed with the defendants' contention that the crimes promulgated and defined under Allied Control Law No. 10 had not included the substantive crime of conspiracy. The tribunal concluded, however, that although it would strike the conspiracy charge from Count One, the related allegation that defendants had also participated in unlawfully forming and executing plans to commit war crimes and crimes against humanity would nevertheless remain as an appropriate criminal charge.

Next, the tribunal addressed one of the most serious criticisms leveled by legal scholars against the Allies war crimes prosecutions—and one of the Nazi judges' alleged defenses to all of the charged crimes—the Allies were seeking to punish the defendants for acts not defined as criminal when the acts were performed. That section of the written judgment is titled in Latin, "*The Ex Post Facto* Principle"—a legal principle that prohibits the application of statutes that define as criminal, acts committed before the law was passed. In the ensuing discussion in the written judgment the tribunal also identified and rejected a related legal principle of international law, "*nullem crimen sine lege*"—a person should not face criminal punishment except for an act that was criminalized by law before the person performed the act.

The tribunal rejected the defendants' arguments under each principle beginning with the defendants' *ex post facto* claim. In an analysis that presaged Brand's later defense of the Nuremberg war crimes prosecutions in academic journals and conferences, the tribunal wrote:

> Under written constitutions the *ex post facto* rule condemns statutes which define as criminal, acts committed before the law was passed, but the *ex post facto* rule cannot apply in the international field as it does under constitutional mandate in the domestic field. Even in the domestic field the prohibition of the rule does not apply to decisions of common law courts, though the question at issue is novel. International law is not the product of statute for the simple reason that there is as yet no world authority empowered to enact statutes of universal application. International law is the product of multipartite treaties, conventions, judicial decisions and customs which have received international acceptance or acquiescence. It would be sheer absurdity to suggest that the *ex post facto* rule, as known to constitutional states, could be applied to a treaty, a custom or a common law decision of an international tribunal, or to the international acquiescence which follows the event. To have attempted to apply the *ex post facto* principle to judicial decisions of common international law would have been to strangle that law at birth.[136]

Regarding the *nullum crimen sine lege* rule the tribunal
began by quoting the interpretation given the rule by the
first International Military Tribunal and set out in that
judgment:

In the first place, it is to be observed that the maxim
nullum crimen sine lege is not a limitation of sovereignty,
but a principle of justice. To assert that it is unjust to
punish those who in defiance of treaties and assurances
have attacked neighboring States without warning is
obviously untrue, for in such circumstances the attacker
must know that he is doing wrong, and so far from being
unjust to punish him, it would be unjust if his wrong were
allowed to go unpunished.[137]

In addition to relying on the first tribunal's reasoning, Brand also
explained in detail in the judgment, why the *nullem crimen sine lege* rule
would not be violated by the Nuremberg prosecutions:

As a principle of justice and fair play, the rule in question
will be given full effect. As applied in the field of
international law that principle requires proof before
conviction that the accused knew or should have known
that in matters of international concern he was guilty of
participation in a rationally organized system of injustice
and persecution shocking to the moral sense of mankind,
and that he knew or should have known that he would be
subject to punishment if caught. Whether it is considered
codification or substantive legislation, no person who
knowingly committed the acts made punishable by
[Control] Law 10 can assert that he did not know that he
would be brought to account for his acts. Notice of intent
to punish was repeatedly given by the only means available
in international affairs, namely the solemn warning of the
governments of the States at war with Germany.[138]

Next, in three paragraphs of the lengthy written judgment, Brand rejected the defendants' desperate plea to avoid punishment based on some form of "judicial immunity" and summarized the iniquitous nature of the Nazi judicial system administered and executed by the defendants:

In view of the conclusive proof of the sinister influence which were in constant interplay between Hitler, his ministers, the Ministry of Justice, the party, the Gestapo, and the courts, we see no merit in the suggestion that Nazi judges are entitled to the benefit of the Anglo-American doctrine of judicial immunity. The doctrine that judges are not personally liable for their judicial actions is based on the concept of an independent judiciary administering impartial justice. Furthermore, it has never prevented the prosecution of a judge for malfeasance in office. If the evidence cited supra does not demonstrate the utter destruction of judicial independence and impartiality, then we 'never writ nor no man proved."[139] The function of the Nazi Courts was judicial only in a limited sense. They more closely resembled administrative tribunals acting under directives from above in a quasi-judicial manner.

In operation, the Nazi system forced the judges into one of two categories. In the first we find the judges who still retained ideals of judicial independence and who administered justice with a measure of impartiality and moderation. Judgments which they rendered were set aside by the employment of the nullity plea and the extraordinary objection. The defendants they sentenced were frequently transferred to the Gestapo on completion of prison terms and were then shot or sent to concentration camps. The judges themselves were threatened and criticized and sometimes removed from office. To this group the defendant Cuhorst belonged. In the other category were the judges who with fanatical zeal enforced the will of the Party with such severity that they experienced no difficulties and little interference from party officials. To this group the defendants Rothaug and Oeschey belonged.[140]

After spending hours reading aloud the factual determinations and evidentiary evaluations set out in the judgment, tribunal members alternated summarizing the evidence against the individual defendants and setting out the reasons supporting a finding of guilt or innocence in each of the following cases.[141]

Franz Schlegelberger

Schlegelberger was the first to learn his fate. According to the tribunal, Schlegelberger had supported Hitler's assumption of authority to dispense life and death without judicial process. The tribunal found that Schlegelberger had through exhortations and directives, contributed significantly to the destruction of judicial independence in Germany. It had been, the tribunal noted, Schlegelberger's signature on the decree of February 7, 1942, that imposed on the Ministry of Justice and its courts the burden of the prosecuting, trying, and disposing of those victimized by Hitler's Night and Fog decree.[142]

According to the tribunal, Schlegelberger had also instituted and supported the processes for persecution of Jews and Poles. Schlegelberger also knew of the pending procedures for the wholesale removal of Jews in Europe and acquiesced in them. He drafted a proposed ordinance "concerning the administration of justice regarding Poles and Jews in the incorporated Eastern territories" that became the basis, with certain modifications and changes, for Germany's Law Against Poles and Jews. Accordingly, the tribunal concluded that Schlegelberger was guilty of participating in the racial persecution of Poles and Jews, and guilty of violating the laws and customs of war by causing the law which he had helped create to be applied in the occupied eastern territories. The tribunal observed that extending such laws into occupied territories directly violated limitations imposed by The Hague Convention.[143]

Next, the tribunal pointed out that in January, 1942, Schlegelberger had issued a decree providing that the Law against Poles and Jews "will be equally applicable with the consent of the public prosecutor to offenses committed before the decree came into force." The tribunal found that the retroactive extension of that discriminatory law into occupied territories could not be justified as a military necessity. Although Schlegelberger had supposedly disapproved "of the revision of sentences" by the police, he had nevertheless personally ordered the murder of the Jew Luftglass at Hitler's request and assured the Fuehrer that he would himself take action if the Fuehrer informed him of other sentences with which the Fuehrer was displeased.[144]

The tribunal described Schlegelberger's defense as "interesting," noting that it was similar to that proffered in some form by most of the other defendants. Among other things, Schlegelberger asserted that the administration of justice in Germany had been under persistent assault by Himmler and other advocates of the police state; the tribunal agreed. Schlegelberger also contended that if the administration of justice had been completely usurped by the lawless forces under Hitler and Himmler, then the last state of the nation would have been worse than the first. In effect, Schlegelberger argued that, had he resigned from his post, a worse individual would have taken his place. Again, the tribunal agreed, observing that, under Otto Thierack—Schlegelberger's successor and one of the early Nazi defendants sentenced to death at the first war crimes tribunal—the police had, in fact gone on to usurp the administration of justice, murdering untold thousands of Jews and political prisoners in the process.[145]

The Justice Case tribunal concluded, however, that Schlegelberger's defense could not be squared with either truth, logic, or the factual circumstances. From the tribunal's perspective, the evidence conclusively illustrated that, in order to maintain the Ministry of Justice in

Hitler's good graces and prevent its utter subjugation by Himmler's police, Schlegelberger and the other defendants who echoed his defense claims had, in fact, willingly taken over the dirty work demanded by the Nazi state. In the end, the tribunal found, the defendants had used the Ministry of Justice as a means for exterminating Jewish and Polish populations, terrorizing the inhabitants of the occupied countries, and wiping out political opposition at home. According to the tribunal, the fact that their program of racial extermination under the guise of law had failed to attain the same scale as that of the pogroms, deportations, and mass police murders, was cold comfort to the survivors of that "'judicial' process and constituted a poor excuse for defendants' actions."[146]

Ultimately, the tribunal described Schlegelberger as a tragic figure who loved intellectual pursuits and scholarship while loathing the evil he had facilitated. In the tribunal's view, Schlegelberger had nevertheless "sold that intellect and that scholarship to Hitler for a mess of political pottage and for the vain hope of personal security." The tribunal went on to find Schlegelberger guilty of war crimes and crimes against humanity under Counts Two and Three of the indictment.[147]

Herbert Klemm

As to defendant Klemm, the tribunal began by finding that as State Secretary for the Ministry of Justice and Deputy Minister in the minister's absence, Klemm's official duties had required his knowledge of operations and policies originating at the Reich's higher levels. Among those policies had been the standardized implementation of abuse in concentration camps, the practice of severe interrogation, persecution, and oppression of Jews, Poles and gypsies, and the basis for the Night and Fog procedures implemented by the Ministry of Justice. According to the tribunal, it was clear from the evidence that Klemm had known of the Jewish persecutions as early as 1940 while serving as a Nazi official in Holland, and was, to some extent, connected to them.[148]

Among other things, the tribunal found that Klemm had known and approved of actions taken to murder inmates at the Sonnenburg penal institution. According to the tribunal, even in Nazi Germany, the clearing of an entire prison and liquidation of 300 inmates could hardly have escaped the Minister of Justice's attention or that of his State Secretary, who was specifically charged with supervising those institutions. In support of that proposition, the tribunal pointed to evidence showing that penal operations and inmate dispositions were clearly a Ministry of Justice function. The tribunal opined that the Ministry of Justice had been, at the time of the Sonnenburg incident, responsible for turning inmates over to the Gestapo for liquidation, and that Klemm had approved the substance of that transaction, if not its details.[149]

The tribunal also pointed out that when Rothenberger was ousted as State Secretary because he was insufficiently brutal, it was Klemm who was chosen to carry on in close cooperation with the Nazi leadership. The tribunal reasoned that because Klemm operated within that inner circle of Nazi war criminals, he must also share responsibility at a high policy level with his dead friend Thierack, (with whom he had lived), and his missing friend Bormann (tried by the IMT in absentia), for the crimes committed by the Reich in the name of justice. The tribunal concluded that Klemm, was guilty of war crimes and crimes against humanity under Counts Two and Three of the Indictment.[150]

Curt Rothenberger

The tribunal's discussion of the evidence against defendant Rothenberger was brief. According to the tribunal, Rothenberger was guilty of taking a minor but consenting part in the Night and Fog program and guilty of aiding and abetting the Reich's program of racial persecution and, notwithstanding his many protestations to the contrary, had materially contributed toward the ultimate subordination of the Ministry of Justice to the arbitrary will of Hitler, his Party minions, and the police. The tribunal concluded that because Rothenberger had participated in corrupting and perverting the German judicial system, he was guilty of war crimes and crimes against humanity under Counts Two and Three of the indictment.[151]

Ernst Lautz

As to Ernst Lautz, evidence in the form of captured German documents established that Lautz had criminally helped enforce the Law against Poles and Jews as part of the Reich's plan for exterminating those disfavored groups. Lautz, the tribunal found, had essentially consented to serve as an accessory to criminal genocide. Lautz was found guilty of violating the laws and customs of war in connection with the prosecutions carried out under the Night and Fog Decree. He was also found guilty of perverting the laws criminalizing treason and high treason under which Poles guilty of petty offenses were executed. The tribunal concluded, however, that proof of Lautz's guilt was not dependent solely on captured documents or the testimony of prosecution witnesses. According to the tribunal, Lautz's own sworn statements justified a finding that he was guilty of war crimes and crimes against humanity under Counts Two and Three of the indictment.[152]

Wolfgang Mettgenberg

Similarly, the tribunal noted that, by his own sworn statements, defendant Mettgenberg had also frankly and fully admitted his connection to Hitler's Night and Fog Decree. The tribunal found that Mettgenberg's own statements demonstrated that he had exercised wide discretion and authority over the mechanics of the Night and Fog program, beginning when a prisoner was arrested in occupied territory, through the prisoner's transfer to Germany, trial, and eventual execution or imprisonment.[153] The tribunal found Mettgenberg guilty beyond a reasonable doubt of war crimes and crimes against humanity under Counts Two and Three of the indictment based on evidence that he had been a principal actor in executing the Night and Fog Decree in violation of international law principles.[154]

Wilhelm von Ammon

Regarding defendant von Ammon, the tribunal noted that the prosecution had introduced into evidence a captured document containing lists of many hundreds of death sentences which had been submitted to the Minister of Justice for review. The cases were classified as either "clear" or "doubtful," with the former greatly outnumbering the latter. As set forth in the captured document, between January 1944 and November 1944, von Ammon had issued 24 reports, each detailing multiple cases in which persons from occupied territories had been sentenced to death under the Night and Fog Decree. Those death sentences had been meted out on an average of more than one every three days during the roughly 10-month period covered in the captured document. The tribunal found von Ammon guilty of war crimes and crimes against humanity under Counts Two and Three of the indictment.[155]

Guenther Joel

In August 1943, defendant Joel became Chief Prosecutor of the German Court of Appeals in Hamm, covering all of Westphalia and the district of Essen. He held that office continually through the war's end. While in that position, Joel administered the Night and Fog program for the Special Courts in Essen until March 1944, when those courts were transferred farther east. The tribunal cited reports showing that Joel had attended conferences both in Hamm and in Belgium on Night and Fog matters, and that his district—in which he was the highest judicial official, and therefore the most responsible, prosecuting authority—was, in area and population, one of the largest in Germany. Joel supervised the senior public prosecutors and their staffs at the Special Courts in Essen, as well as all the prosecutors directly assigned to his office. The Special Courts in Essen, the tribunal noted, had tried more Night and Fog cases than all the other courts in Germany combined, cases for which Joel had direct responsibility. The tribunal also noted that Joel had possessed knowledge of the concentration camps and their conditions as early as 1937. Between September 1942 and March 1943, Joel reviewed 105 death sentences passed by courts in the incorporated Eastern territories and in most of those cases had given final approval for execution. The evidence showed that, as a highly placed official in the Ministry of Justice and liaison between the Ministry and the SS, Joel had been given extensive access to information concerning the Law against Jews and Poles and had exercised far-reaching power in its execution. The tribunal therefore concluded that Joel had actively taken part in the persecution and extermination of those peoples.[156]

Concerning Joel's membership in the SS and SD, the tribunal concluded that the evidence demonstrated beyond a reasonable doubt that he had retained his membership in those organizations with full knowledge of their criminal character. The tribunal found Joel guilty of war crimes and crimes against humanity under Counts Two and Three of the indictment. As to Count Four of the indictment, the tribunal also found Joel guilty of membership in a criminal organization, reasoning that no one possessing Joel's intimate contacts with the Reich Security Main Office, the SS, the SD, and the Gestapo could possibly have been ignorant regarding the nature of those organizations.[157]

Oswald Rothaug

Despite defendant Rothaug's protestations that the judgments he had rendered in court had all been based solely on the evidence introduced therein, the tribunal found that in innumerable cases, Rothaug's decisions had been made well before the conclusion of a trial and, in many instances, publicly or privately announced before trial had even commenced. Rothaug, the tribunal found, had regularly formed his opinions from dubious records submitted to him before trial and through that methodology, had made his court an instrument of terror feared and hated throughout Germany.[158]

Based on evidence elicited from Rothaug's closest associates as well as his victims, the tribunal found that Rothaug had come to personify Nazi cruelty as a particularly sadistic and evil adjudicator. According to the tribunal, in any civilized judicial system, Rothaug would have been impeached and removed from office or convicted of malfeasance by virtue of the malevolence with which he administered injustice. The tribunal easily concluded that Rothaug was guilty of crimes against humanity under Count Three of the indictment.[159]

Rudolf Oeschey

For defendant Oeschey, the tribunal began by pointing out that Rothaug had often been considered the worst Special Court judge in Germany, in part because he would frequently inform defendants during their trials that they were to be exterminated. After Rothaug was transferred to Berlin, however, Oeschey would eventually surpass him in spitefulness of manner. As an example, the tribunal cited the trial of some foreign youths who had fought with other boys from the Nuremberg Hitler Youth Home. Dr. Mueller—a prosecution witness—characterized the actions of the young defendants as a series of harmless pranks, the work of children seeking to provoke street fights with other children who happened to be members of the Hitler Youth. Oeschey, however, held that the defendants' actions had constituted a resistance movement and sentenced several of the boys to death.

Oeschey was also charged under Count Four of the indictment with being a member of the Party Leadership Corps at the regional level, a position that fell within the definition of memberships declared criminal by the first tribunal. Oeschey had been provisionally commissioned to direct the Nazi party's legal office in the Franconia region and served in that official capacity for some time. Oeschey testified that from 1940 to 1942 he had been a member of the Party Leadership and was solely responsible for the region's legal office as section chief. According to the tribunal, the Leadership Corps to which Oeschey admitted belonging had played no small part in the economic and political persecution of the Jews beginning shortly after the Nazis came to power. The machinery of the Leadership Corps had also been utilized in attempts to deprive captured Allied airmen of the protections to which they were entitled under the Geneva Convention. To underscore Oeschey's knowledge of the Leadership Corps' activities, the tribunal highlighted the fact that Oeschey had joined the Nazi Party in December 1931 and was head of the Lawyers League for Franconia and a judicial officer of considerable importance within that region. These offices, the tribunal noted, had subsequently provided additional sources of information as to Oeschey's crimes.[160] In pronouncing Oeschey guilty of crimes against humanity and membership in a criminal organization under Counts Three and Four of the indictment, the tribunal expressly found that "[i]n view of the sadistic attitude and conduct of the defendant, we know of no just reason for any mitigation of punishment."[161]

Josef Altstötter

ALTSTÖTTER

In passing judgment on Josef Altstötter, the tribunal observed that he had joined and retained his membership in the SS on a voluntary basis and took considerable interest in his SS rank and honors. According to the tribunal, the evidence in that regard left no doubt that the brutal treatment of concentration camp inmates was carried out as a matter of general SS policy that viewed inmates as racial inferiors to be treated only with contempt. Altstötter was a member of the SS at the time of the November 1938 pogrom known as "Crystal Week," in which the SS was found to have had an important role. The tribunal reasoned that regardless of whether Altstötter had directly taken part or approved of such activities, he would nevertheless have known of the role played by the organization of which he was an officer. As a lawyer, he knew that in October of 1940, the SS had been placed beyond reach of the law, and that under the 13th Amendment to the German Citizenship Law, Jews were to be turned over to the police and deprived of any legal protections they had previously enjoyed. Altstötter was also aware of the legal provisions made for police confiscation of Jewish properties upon the owners' deaths.[162] Ultimately, the tribunal concluded that Altstötter was guilty of membership in a criminal organization under Count Four of the Indictment, but found him not guilty of war crimes and crimes against humanity set out in Counts Two and Three.[163]

To the surprise of many who observed the tribunal proceedings, the tribunal found four of the defendants not guilty of the charges against them: Hans Petersen, Paul Barnickel, Guenther Nebelung, and Hermann Cuhorst. Regarding defendants Petersen, Barnickel, and Nebelung, the tribunal simply commented that the evidence before it had not convinced the tribunal of the defendants' guilt beyond a reasonable doubt as to any of the charges alleged against them.[164]

Regarding Cuhorst, however, the tribunal rendered a lengthier disposition. It began by noting that although Cuhorst was charged under Counts Two, Three and Four of the indictment, no evidence had been introduced to substantiate the charges under Counts Two and Four, requiring Cuhorst to be found not guilty on those counts.[165] As to Count Three however, the tribunal faced a problem considerably more complicated. According to the tribunal, many affidavits and much of the testimony on the record had clearly demonstrated that Cuhorst was a fanatical Nazi and a ruthless judge, with evidence detailing the arbitrary, unfair, and unjudicial manner in which he conducted his trials. Some of that evidence had been weakened on cross examination, the tribunal noted, but the general picture of Cuhorst as an untoward adjudicator was the one accepted by the tribunal.[166]

That said, however, the tribunal noted that the allegations linking him with crimes under Count Three revolved primarily around his alleged connection to incidents of Polish persecution. The tribunal observed that unfortunately, the relevant records contained at the Stuttgart Special Court had been destroyed when the Stuttgart Palace of Justice was burned, among them, the records of cases tried by Cuhorst. As a result, the tribunal concluded that it could not find beyond a reasonable doubt that Cuhorst was guilty of inflicting racially based punishments in his court, or that he had used the discriminatory provisions of the Decree Against Poles and Jews to the detriment of the Poles whom he had tried.[167]

The tribunal also observed that, although Cuhorst had followed a misguided fanaticism, certain things could be said in his favor. He had been severely criticized by defendant Klemm for his leniency in a number of cases and had apparently been relieved of his judicial duties because he had failed to conform to the Reich's demands on the German judiciary. In the tribunal's view, it had not been commissioned to try or condemn the conscience of those charged before it based merely on conduct that the tribunal found foreign to its own concept of justice. Based on the evidence adduced at trial, the tribunal concluded that Cuhorst had not been proved guilty beyond a reasonable doubt and also acquitted him of crimes against humanity.[168]

Although the tribunal acquitted Cuhorst of the charges against him, that was not the end of his troubles. Cuhorst was later arrested by local German authorities in 1948 and tried in denazification proceedings.[169] Found guilty, Cuhorst was sentenced to four years in a labor camp, had his property confiscated, and was placed under occupational restriction. He was released from confinement in 1950.[170]

After rendering judgment concerning the defendants' guilt, Brand concluded that phase of the proceeding reading from the judgment:

> Concerning these defendants who have been found guilty, our conclusions are not based solely on the facts which we have set forth in the separate discussions of the individual defendants. In the course of nine months devoted to the trial and consideration of this case, we have reached conclusions based on evidence and observation of the defendants which cannot fully be documented within the limitations of time and space allotted to us. As we have said, the defendants are not charged with specific overt acts against named victims. They are charged with criminal

participation of governmentally organized atrocities and persecutions unmatched in the annals of history. Our judgments are based on a consideration of all of the evidence which tends to throw light upon the part which these defendants played in the entire tragic drama. We shall, in pronouncing sentence, give due consideration to circumstances of mitigation and to the proven character and motives of the respective defendants.[171]

Justice Brand reads aloud the lengthy judgment.

CHAPTER THIRTEEN: SENTENCING THE JUSTICE CASE DEFENDANTS

THE DAY AFTER THE tribunal finished reading its verdicts as to each defendant, Justice Brand announced the tribunal's sentences. The severity of those sentences appeared to have been rendered according to the enormity of each defendant's crimes.[172]

Four of the defendants, Schlegelberger, Rothaug, Oeschey, and Klemm, were sentenced to life in prison. All four, however, were released early. Schlegelberger was released after only three years of incarceration. He lived until 1970 and received a generous monthly pension until his death. Burt Lancaster's portrayal of Judge Ernst Janning in the movie *Judgment at Nuremberg*, was based loosely on the prosecution of Schlegelberger and Rothaug. Rothaug was released from prison in 1956 and died in 1967; Oeschey was released in 1956 and died in 1980; Klemm was released in 1956 and died in 1961.[173]

Another four defendants, Lautz, Mettgenberg, von Ammon, and Joel were each sentenced to 10 years in prison, with credit for the period spent in pre-trial confinement. Lautz was released in 1951 and died in 1979; Mettgenberg died in 1950; von Ammon was released in 1951 and died in 1992; Joel was released in 1951 and died in 1978.[174]

Two of the defendants received lesser sentences. Rothenberger was sentenced to seven years in prison, with credit for the period of time spent in pre-trial confinement. He was released in 1950 and died in 1959. Altstötter was sentenced to five years in prison with credit for his period of pre-trial confinement. He was released in 1950 and died in 1979.[175]

CHAPTER FOURTEEN: RETURNING TO THE OREGON SUPREME COURT

THERE IS NO RECORD of when or how the Brands traveled back to Oregon. However, in one of Irene Brand's last letters home, she wrote that Justice Brand had been asked to stay and serve on one of the upcoming tribunals. In explaining why her husband had refused the offer, Mrs. Brand noted his need to return to Oregon in order to stand for re-election in May 1948.[176] Justice Brand had no opponent in the 1948 election, and was reelected unopposed again in 1954.[177]

After serving as Justice Brand's secretary/law clerk in the Justice Case, Hattie Bratzel served as a court reporter in two other Nuremberg tribunals. Returning to Oregon, she completed law school, practiced law in Salem, OR, and was elected Marion County District Attorney in 1956 and 1960, the first woman in Oregon elected to such a position.

Hattie Bratzel, for her part, did not immediately return home. Instead, she stayed in Germany serving as a court reporter for two subsequent tribunals. When Bratzel eventually returned to Oregon,

FOR HONEST, FEARLESS AND
EFFICIENT SERVICE
ELECT
Hattie J. Bratzel
As Your
DISTRICT ATTORNEY
FOR MARION COUNTY
REPUBLICAN NOMINEE
Election November 6, 1956
Integrity, Experience, Ability

Hattie Bratzel for District Attorney campaign flyer

she completed law school, passed the Oregon State Bar Examination in 1951, and married Howard Kremen, described by one Salem newspaper as one of Salem's most eligible bachelors. In 1956 she was elected Marion County District Attorney, the first woman in Oregon history to hold such an office. Although reelected in 1960, she lost her bid for a third term in 1964.[178]

In February 1948, soon after Brand returned to his judicial duties on the Oregon Supreme Court, he told *The Oregonian* newspaper that he thought that the Justice Case had accomplished several objectives, the least of which, according to Brand, had been the punishment of very guilty men. More important, in Brand's view, had been the principle demonstrated to the German people of absolute fairness in a criminal trial, and the publication of facts concerning Nazi tyranny and its effect on the German judicial system. The latter point was particularly important from Brand's perspective because, for the first time, a full factual record in an international criminal matter had been established for historical purposes through the judicial process. Instead of being gagged or summarily delt with at trial, all defendants had been encouraged and aided in providing evidence on their own behalf. That resulted in the historical record of events being accurately and immediately established. According to Brand, the Justice Case had also advanced rules of law pertaining to individuals in international affairs. "[A]ll the defendants and their counsel," Brand told *The Oregonian* "were satisfied that they had a fair trial."[179]

Oregon Supreme Court records reveal that Brand returned to the court in time to hear cases on the court's January 1948 docket. Just two months later, the court released five lengthy opinions in civil cases from that docket, all authored by Justice Brand.[180] In the next 10 years, Brand would author opinions in 218 of the court's cases, sometimes writing for the majority, sometimes concurring with a decision, and sometimes dissenting. Remarkably, in writing his majority opinions Brand rarely took more than two months after oral arguments to produce and publish the court's decision. Of the many opinions that Brand wrote during that 10-year period, 20 involved criminal matters. Those criminal opinions addressed issues concerning the sufficiency and admissibility of evidence, false swearing, murder, vehicular manslaughter, assault, conversion of public funds, criminal fraud, contributing to the delinquency of a minor, abortion, arson, and various sub-constitutional questions of criminal procedure. It is worth noting that Justice Brand's service on the Oregon Supreme Court occurred before the United States Supreme Court ruled in the 1960s that federal Bill of Rights protections,—specifically the Fourth, Fifth, Sixth, and Eighth Amendments to the United States Constitution—applied to the states through the Fourteenth Amendment to the United States Constitution. Consequently, Brand had little occasion to consider or apply those aspects of constitutional law in his decision-making.

Of the 20 criminal case opinions that Justice Brand authored upon his return to Oregon, two are particularly interesting: *State v. Long*, and *State v. Sack*. Both were majority opinions in death penalty cases. Together, they represented the first two such matters to come before the court with Brand again on the bench.

In *State v. Long*, the evidence established that the defendant Wayne Long had been released from the Oregon State Penitentiary on June 14, 1950, at nine o'clock in the morning.[181] Sometime after ten o'clock that night, he was seen in Portland getting into a Ford pickup truck owned and driven by Walter Rucker. At about 6:15 in the morning of the next day, Long was seen driving the Ford pickup alone. Several hours later, he arrived at the First National Bank, in Southeast Portland, entered it, and came out shortly thereafter with a rifle in one hand and shopping bags in the other. An FBI agent present at the scene ordered him to stop; Long shot the agent but while running to Rucker's pickup truck, was himself shot and taken into custody by other FBI agents. At three o'clock on the same day, Rucker's body was found near Eagle Fern Park in an isolated part of Clackamas County; he had been shot in the head. Justice Brand concluded the recitation of those facts by noting for the reader: "From the release of the defendant at the penitentiary to the moment of his capture, only 25 hours had elapsed."

Writing for a unanimous court, Justice Brand affirmed the defendant's murder conviction and death sentence. In doing so, he noted among other things, the court's displeasure with the timeliness of defense counsel's objections to the prosecution's use of "other crimes" evidence at Long's trial, i.e., the bank robbery and shooting of a federal agent. In what was certainly a teachable moment for Oregon legal practitioners concerning proper objection practice, Brand wrote:

> The admissibility of the evidence on which the prosecution commented can only be ascertained by a careful review of the entire case. At this point defense counsel objected 'to any further testimony along this line.' The objection was overruled. It will be observed that the objection was not made to the testimony last quoted, nor was there a motion to strike. In this case, and throughout the transcript of testimony, counsel for the defendant followed the practice of waiting until a question had been asked and an answer given, and then objecting to any further testimony. This court does not look with favor upon objections made, or upon motions to strike, when the objection could have been, but was not, made to the question asked before the answer has been given.

Regarding, the admissibility of that evidence, Justice Brand opined:

> No one can read the transcript of testimony and not be convinced that every act of the defendant, from his release

at the door of the penitentiary to the moment of his arrest, was part of a plan, actually carried out, to equip himself with weapons, ammunition, dark glasses, and a get-away car, for the purpose of accomplishing a successful bank robbery. The evidence tended to indicate that the killing of the owner of the car, for the purpose of securing it, was an integral part of the transaction and was motivated by the intention to commit the subsequent robbery.

Justice Brand concluded the opinion: "This being a capital case, the court has gone through the evidence in minute detail, notwithstanding the defective procedure by which the issues were raised. We conclude that there was sufficient evidence to go to the jury on every issue raised by the indictment, and that no prejudicial error was committed." Six months after the court issued its opinion, Wayne Long was executed in Oregon's gas chamber.

In the second murder case, *State v. Sack*, the defendant had been charged with murdering his third wife, having previously been implicated in three other homicide investigations, two of which involved the deaths of his first two wives. In both cases, the defendant had obtained life insurance proceeds from those deaths. The defendant's first wife had died in a suspicious fire.[182] His second wife had died from a bullet to the brain. The defendant had been charged with murdering his second wife, but had been defended by the famous lawyer, Clarence Darrow.[183] The jury in that case ultimately found the defendant insane and he was committed to an asylum. The defendant was subsequently accused of murdering his third wife by drugging her and placing her in the trunk of his car where she died of asphyxiation. On appeal, the defendant raised multiple assignments of error involving evidence of the couple's fraught marital relationship, their individual finances, and the cause of the third wife's death. Again writing for a unanimous court, Justice Brand analyzed and rejected each of the defendant's claims. Consistent with his judicial tendency to evaluate all the evidence in terms of

overall fairness to the defendant, Justice Brand concluded his opinion
by stating:

> We are well aware of the gravity of the charge against
> this defendant, and of the consequences of the verdict
> and judgment in this case. A careful examination
> of the extensive record convinces the court that the
> defendant was given a fair trial. We have found no error
> prejudicial to his rights. The jury was warranted, under
> the evidence, in finding the defendant guilty of deliberate
> and premeditated murder as charged in the indictment.
> The penalty has been fixed by unanimous verdict. The
> judgment pronounced thereon is affirmed.

Although the defendant Sack's death sentence was affirmed, there
is no record that he was executed in Oregon.

Justice Brand also wrote in three other criminal cases that merit
some examination: *State v. Hansen, State v. Caputo,* and *State v. Cahill.*
In *Hansen,* the defendant had been accused of murdering her husband
by backing over him with their car as he lay intoxicated on the garage
floor.[184] A jury subsequently found the defendant guilty of first-degree
murder, and she was sentenced to life imprisonment. On appeal, she
challenged the sufficiency of the evidence against her, as well as an
allegedly erroneous jury instruction. The majority opinion authored by
Justice Lusk rejected the defendant's sufficiency of the evidence argument but agreed that the challenged jury instruction had been wrong
and the court remanded the case for a new trial. Justices Rossman and
Latourette filed separate dissents, each arguing that the evidence had,
as a matter of law, not been enough to have the first-degree murder
charge submitted to the jury. Justice Brand filed a separate opinion
concurring with the majority and pointing out the limitations imposed
on the court by the Oregon Constitution. He wrote:

I concur in the decision and in the able opinion of Mr. Justice LUSK in his dealing with the facts and the law. Were I a juror duly empaneled and sworn to try the case in the circuit court and upon the present record I should no doubt be impressed by the argument in behalf of the defendant's case which appears in the dissenting opinions. Being mindful, however, of the limitations imposed by the constitution upon the scope of judicial review, I am unmoved by the recital of the testimony which is suggestive of innocence but which ignores much that tends to show guilt. My sympathies are strongly enlisted in this case, but it is of the essence of the judicial function that judgment must not be swayed by interest. * * * no fact tried by a jury shall be otherwise re-examined in any court of this State, unless the court can affirmatively say there is no evidence to support the verdict. * * * Constitution of Oregon, Art VII, § 3. Stripped of fine-spun argument concerning the "theory of the case", the question which the jury decided and which only a jury should decide is—did the defendant kill her husband? I am unable to 'affirmatively say there is no evidence to support the verdict.'

In *State v. Caputo*, the defendant was convicted of contributing to the delinquency of a minor female by engaging in sexual intercourse with her.[185] The court affirmed the defendant's conviction, stating that: "[a]lthough the child had indulged in somewhat indiscriminate sexual intercourse before meeting the defendant, there is substantial evidence that she had not therefore become a prostitute for pay. In truth the jury was entitled to find that she became more delinquent by reason of the defendant's acts." However, Justice Brand penned a separate concurrence to clarify prior statements made by the court regarding the elements of the crime of contributing to the delinquency of a minor:

The defendant relies upon certain language found in *State v. Moore, supra*. Our discussion in that case related, not to the indictment, but to the evidence. We said: '* * * Of course, it is further necessary to prove that the act or acts so established manifestly tended to cause the child to become a delinquent child. In other words, it is necessary to establish by the evidence: (1) one or more of the acts of misconduct specifically alleged, and (2) that such act or acts manifestly tended to cause the child to become a delinquent child.' The case was decided upon the ground that the specific act charged against the defendant was not proven. We did not intend to intimate that there is, as it were, an open season as to any child who has once become delinquent. It is unthinkable that the legislature intended that the waywardness of the child should be a defense to a man who attempts to lead her into a life of commercialized degeneracy.

In *State v. Cahill*, the defendant was convicted of converting public funds to his own personal use.[186] On appeal, Justice Brand wrote for the majority, holding that, although the trial court had erred in admitting the testimony of three handwriting experts, that error did not require reversal of the defendant's conviction. In affirming the trial court's decision, Justice Brand relied on Article VII, section 3 of the Oregon Constitution which provides, in part: "If the [S]upreme [C]ourt shall be of the opinion, after consideration of all the matters thus submitted, that the judgment of the court appealed from was such as should have been rendered in the case, such judgment shall be affirmed, notwithstanding any error committed during the trial* * *."

Consistent with his understanding of the court's case review power under the Oregon Constitution, Justice Brand concluded his opinion by stating simply: "A trial is no longer a game of wits; it is a search for truth and justice. We have found truth in the evidence of the prosecution and justice in the verdict of the jury and judgment of the court. We have examined the other assignments of error and find them without merit. The judgment of conviction is affirmed on the authority of Article VII, § 3 of the Constitution of Oregon."

Although Justice Brand was profoundly affected by his service in Germany, there was no discernable change in his judicial philosophy or approach to deciding cases following his return from Nuremberg. Justice Brand's opinions generally defy attempts to classify him or his judicial philosophy as conservative or liberal as those terms are understood today. Rather, Justice Brand's opinions both before and after Nuremberg consistently demonstrated a loftier decisions-making ethic: study the applicable law deeply, respect its rule, and maintain an unwavering fidelity to judicial restraint.

On a more granular level, however, certain traits regarding Brand's particular approach to appellate review in criminal matters do indeed emerge from Brand's opinions. First, throughout his tenure on Oregon's highest court, Justice Brand was sensitive to the adage "justice delayed is justice denied" and produced opinions with enviable speed. Second, his opinions reflected his broad experience in a plethora of legal matters, his intelligence, his curiosity, and his sophisticated approach to thinking and writing about national or international affairs. Third, all of Brand's opinions, whatever the legal subject, demonstrated a powerful mind predisposed to careful thought and effective persuasion. Finally, his opinions frequently revealed both a scrupulous concern for fairness and a compelling sensitivity to his judicial duty under Article VII, section 3 of the Oregon Constitution: to determine in each of the court's cases whether a "judgment shall be affirmed, notwithstanding any error committed during the trial."[187]

After his return from Nuremberg, Justice Brand was elected twice more to the court, serving on the Oregon Supreme Court for another 10 years, two of which as its chief justice. On June 8, 1958, *The Oregonian* newspaper reported Justice Brand's retirement from the bench. At the time Brand retired, Oregon's highest court was experiencing public pressure over the court's backlog of undecided cases. During

an interview on the occasion of his retirement, Brand addressed that
issue and opined that changing the way supreme court justices were
selected in Oregon would help to reduce that backlog. Brand noted that
two recent appointees to the court had been forced by circumstances
to begin election campaigns almost immediately after their appoint-
ments—activities that greatly reduced the time that the new justices
could have devoted to deciding cases and writing opinions. In place
of the "popular vote" system then mandated by the Oregon Constitution, Brand advocated for adoption of the so-called Missouri System
as a superior means of selecting and retaining Oregon Supreme Court
justices. Brand explained that under the Missouri System,

> ...supreme court justices are appointed by the governor
> from a list of qualified lawyers selected by a nonpartisan
> commission of lawyers and laymen. The term of office is
> 12 years [as opposed to the six-year term mandated by
> the Oregon Constitution]. They are subject to recall by
> popular vote at stated intervals when they 'run against'
> their record. The vote is taken thus: 'Shall Judge ___ of the
> ___ Court be retained in office? Yes [   ] or No [   ].'[188]

According to Brand: "Judicial office must be separated from partisan politics. Our present system has not wholly succeeded in accomplishing this result. The Missouri System would be an improvement in
this respect." In seeking to change Oregon's selection process for state
supreme court justices, Brand rejected any notion that the "age of the
justices is responsible for the court's backlog of cases." Instead, Brand
defended his colleagues, telling *The Oregonian*:

> "The people of Oregon need not hope and should not
> expect to find in the future any judges who are more
> devoted or more industrious than those of whom I
> speak.... The [backlog of undecided cases] will not
> be solved by listening to the propaganda of ambitious

candidates for high office who would try to convince the public that the problem will be solved by displacing a few elderly judges and substituting youth and inexperience.'

Brand went on to assure Oregonians throughout the state of the court's continued vibrancy and the national respect it enjoyed as a judicial institution: "The people of Oregon have had a strong Supreme Court whose decisions are cited and respected by courts throughout the nation and by legal scholars."[189] Sixty-five years later Oregon still elects its Supreme Court justices by state-wide popular vote.

CHAPTER FIFTEEN: THE FINAL YEARS

THE NUREMBERG WAR CRIMES trials were not free from criticism. For example, no less than United States Supreme Court Chief Justice Harlan Fiske Stone, expressed irritation that Justice Jackson's presence at Nuremberg had taken him away from the Court, as well as doubts about the fairness of the Nuremberg tribunals:

> [Chief United States prosecutor] Jackson is away conducting his high-grade lynching party in Nuremberg. I don't mind what he does to the Nazis, but I hate to see the pretense that he is running a court and proceeding according to common law. This is a little too sanctimonious a fraud to meet my old-fashioned ideas.

In a private letter he would also write: "… I wonder how some of those who preside at the trials would justify some of the acts of their own governments if they were placed in the status of the accused."[190]

Another frequent criticism leveled at the Nuremberg trials was expressed concisely by United States Supreme Court Justice William O. Douglas, who commented: "Law was created *ex post facto* to suit the passion and clamor of the time."[191]

In early 1948, Iowa Supreme Court Justice Charles F. Wennerstrum, who presided over the seventh Nuremberg tribunal known as the Hostages Case, also expressed his disillusionment with the process soon after it was completed: "If I had known seven months ago what I know today, I would never have come here," he declared immediately after sentencing the defendants. "The high ideals announced as the motives for creating these tribunals have not been evident."[192]

Brand promptly responded to Wennerstrum's comments by writing several newspaper articles and giving a speech to the American Bar Association's International and Comparative Law Section. In his speech, he stated unequivocally that "[n]o defendant tried in the criminal courts of the United States has received a trial in which the court and prosecution have so completely protected his every right as did the defendants at [Nuremberg]."[193]

Roughly a year after his return to Oregon, Brand authored an extensive article in the *Oregon Law Review* entitled "Crimes Against Humanity and the Nuremberg Trials."[194] In his article, Brand acknowledged that he had drafted the extensive Justice Case judgment, explained the historic basis for the Crimes Against Humanity charges at Nuremberg, and explained how that crime had been applied to the Nuremberg defendants, who had all been so charged. Brand's article advanced two points to counter the broad criticisms leveled at the Nuremberg trials, as well as claims that the proceedings had involved *ex post facto* applications of law. First, Brand set out in detail all the procedural rights afforded the defendants: notice of the charges against them, the presumption of their innocence, proof of guilt beyond a reasonable doubt, their right to testify, and their right to cross-examine any witness called by the prosecution. Second, Brand wrote:

> If the critics who have expressed theoretical opposition
> to the [Nuremberg] trials had been placed in positions
> of government responsibility they would have found
> themselves painfully close to the horns of a factual
> dilemma. The men who had been chiefly instrumental
> in the Nazi rise to power and in the terrorism and
> bloodshed which had engulfed the world were alive and
> in Germany, and within the power of the victors. They
> must either be left free or they must be imprisoned or
> executed. It was unthinkable that they be permitted to
> go at large to organize underground resistance among
> millions of convinced Nazis who still populate Germany.

The choice then was between fair trial on the one hand, or imprisonment or execution without trial on the other. The critics who claimed that the trials were not truly judicial assert that it would have been better to have shot the defendants upon the orders of the military than to have followed the procedure which was adopted. Their argument is that it is better to execute men without any law or trial than to punish them under retroactive law providing for fair trial of the issues under law. In the ten [Nuremberg] cases already tried, defendants have been convicted, but twenty-three have been found not guilty. How would those who advocated execution without trial have handled the cases of the twenty-three? Would they have hanged them? Or, if not, then by what means other than fair trial could they have determined guilt or innocence? I think it may safely be left to the conscience of mankind to decide which procedure was the more humane or the more just.[195]

Brand also argued that the *ex post facto* rule had no application in the Justice Case and, in any event, had not been violated by the Nuremberg prosecutions. In that regard, Brand wrote as he had in the Justice Case judgment:

Under written constitutions the *ex post facto* rule condemns statutes which define as criminal acts committed before the statutes were passed, but the *ex post facto* rule cannot apply in the international field as it does under constitutional mandate in the domestic field. * * * International law is a product of multipartite treaties, conventions, judicial decisions, and customs which have received international tribunal, or to the international acquiescence. It would be sheer absurdity to suggest that the *ex post facto* rule, as known to constitutional states, could be applied to a treaty, a custom, or a common-law decision of an international tribunal, or to the international acquiescence which follows the event.[196]

That said, Brand added, that the *ex post facto* principle had nevertheless been adhered to at the Nuremberg trials:

> As a principle of justice and fair play, the [*ex post facto*]
> rule was given full effect. As applied in the field of
> international law that principle requires proof before
> conviction that the accused knew or should have known
> that in matters of international concern he was guilty
> of participation in a nationally organized system of
> injustice and persecution shocking to the moral sense
> of mankind, and he knew or should have known that
> he would be subject to punishment if caught. Whether
> it be considered codification or substantive legislation,
> no person who knowingly committed the acts made
> punishable by Control Council Law No. 10 can assert he
> did not know that he would be brought to account for his
> acts. Notice of intent to punish was repeatedly given by
> the only means available in international affairs, namely,
> the solemn warning of the governments of states at war
> with Germany. Not only were the defendants warned of
> swift retribution by the express declaration of the Allies at
> Moscow of October 30, 1943[,] [l]ong prior to the Second
> World War the principle of personal responsibility has
> been recognized.[197]

In addition to his *Oregon Law Review* article, Brand began work
on a book, with the working title, "Nazi Justice." Unfortunately, it was
never completed.[198] Although only 75 pages of that manuscript remain
today, they reflect Brand's efforts to do more than simply recount his
experiences in Nuremberg, despite the impact that those experiences
had on him as a human being and legal professional. Instead, Brand
sought to initially trace the origins and rise of Nazism in Germany. A
passage in the preface to the manuscript demonstrates Brand's intent
to give a broader and more profound meaning to the Justice Case:

In truth the process in which we were to participate was
unique in history. To the contemplative mind the scene
in the bombed and shattered Palace of Justice was itself
pregnant with meaning. Here was a strange dramatization
of the conflict between two systems of thought; two
ways of life. I intend no false humility in saying that on
the bench sat 'garden variety' American judges, trained
in the exercise of power but only within limits fixed by
constitution, statute and custom. Traditionally we did not
make, but only discovered the law. In criminal cases we
told juries about the law but they told us about the facts
of guilt or innocence. Precedent was a ponderous force.
Arbitrary power was anathema. In the words of Lord
Coke we were 'under God and the law,' yet despite all
this we wore the invisible crown of judicial independence.
Within our powers we were free from political control.
Before us in the dock sat high Nazi officials whose
chief, the Reich Minister of Justice, had been expressly
empowered by Hitler to 'deviate from any existing
law.' Here were judges who had exercised immense
discretionary power—far greater than was ever vested in
an American jurist. Expediency, not justice, was their rule
of decision. They held life and death in the palm of the
hand. Yet, with all their power they had lost the crowning
glory of a judge, judicial independence. In a word, judges
who had been above the law were to be tried by other
judges who were under law. As court convened, the
contrasts in the courtroom were symbolic of the profound
conflict between the political philosophy of America and
the Nazi 'Zeit Geist.'[199]

In Nuremberg, Brand had met and become friends with Harold
Sebring, a member of the tribunal presiding over what came to be
known as the Medical Case. During the war, the defendants in the
Medical Case had performed dangerous, deadly, and excruciatingly

painful experiments on Jews, prisoners of war, and other concentration camp inmates. Both the Medical Case and the Justice Case were tried at roughly the same time in separate Palace of Justice courtrooms.

During his judicial career, Sebring had served as a justice and chief justice of the Florida Supreme Court. By 1958, when Brand retired from the Oregon Supreme Court, Sebring was Dean of Stetson University College of Law, a small and relatively new law school located in Gulf-port, Florida. Learning of Brand's retirement, Sebring invited him to teach at Stetson.

In 1958, at the age of 72, Brand accepted the position offered by his friend and began teaching Constitutional Law, Torts, and Municipal Corporations on Florida's gulf coast. In addition to those teaching duties, Brand and Sebring co-advised the school's moot court team that participated in the National Moot Court Competition. Brand taught at Stetson until 1963, when he returned to Salem, Oregon to practice law with his son Thomas.

In 2013, Bruce R. Jacob, professor and dean emeritus at Stetson, as well as a former student at the institution from 1957 to 1959, delivered remarks at the St. Petersburg, Florida Holocaust Museum about Brand's and Sebring's experiences in Nuremberg. Jacob also provided his audience with observations of those men drawn from his time as their student. Those remarks were published in 2015 by the *Stetson Law Review* in an article titled "Judges At Nuremberg: Stetson's Connection To The War Crimes Trials."[200]

JAMES TENNEY BRAND
Professor of Law; A.B., Oberlin College;
LL.B., Harvard University; LL.D., Willamette University; Presiding Judge, Major
War Criminals Trials, Nurenburg, Germany; former Chief Justice, Supreme Court
of Oregon.

Professor James Tenney Brand,
Stetson College of Law, 1958

At Stetson, Brand and Irene, lived on the first floor of a former hotel in which some of the rooms had been converted into apartments. According to Dean Jacob, because Brand lived and worked on the Stetson campus, his students came to know him intimately as a teacher, mentor, and friend. Dean Jacob described Brand as a humble scholar, possessing enormous integrity, "extremely friendly, likeable and highly regarded by everyone who knew [him]." Jacob's law review article contains a statement about Brand, from one of his former students, United States District Judge Elizabeth Kovachevich. That statement highlights the personal and professional qualities described by Dean Jacob:

When I graduated from law school, Justice Brand and his wife did me the great honor of coming to my home in St. Petersburg and dining with me and my parents. It was a memorable evening of warm and generous conversation with a lovely couple and a man that I have admired as a gallant gentleman and premier jurist. I could never have imagined that I would be privileged, by the people of this

[S]tate and this country, to become a jurist myself. I have
never [forgotten] the example of men like Justice James
T. Brand who knew how to wear the robe and to be so
humane while doing it. [T]hose who were his students
were blessed to study constitutional law with him.[201]

On September 20, 1961, the frontpage headline of *The Oregonian*
newspaper read, "Film Portrays Oregon Judge Who Heard Nuremberg
Trial."[202] Below the headline were large photos of actor Spencer Tracy
and Justice Brand. The article began:

> The cloak of fame, Hollywood model, swathes the
> shoulders of State Supreme Court Justice James T. Brand,
> and the noted Oregon jurist is undergoing the experience
> with a somewhat bemused attitude of elation and
> apprehension, slightly tinged with downright unease.
>
> The heady Southern California exposure is a result of
> Judge Brand's real life leading role in the great drama of
> the mid-20th century, the Nuremberg trials of 1947, which
> has been made into a movie by Producer Stanley Kramer
> and is scheduled for a world premier in West Berlin Dec.
> 14 in Kongress Halle.
>
> Spencer Tracy plays the role of the distinguished Oregon
> judge, and because the film is a fictionalized dramatization
> and not a newsreel commentary, he is listed as Daniel
> Haywood, "a self-effacing judge from Maine, a 'down East'
> character who is honest and a man of fierce integrity.[203]

The Oregonian

Film Portrays Oregon Judge Who Heard Nuernberg Trials

REAL LIFE Judge James T. Brand, now an Oregon Supreme Court Justice, is played by white-maned Spencer Tracy in the film "Judgment at Nuernberg." Tracy portrays jurist brought to Germany to try former Nazi judges, as Brand did in 1947. Film is not a documentary.

JUSTICE BRAND, who is not without resemblance to Spencer Tracy, as he appears today. He was the presiding judge of the series of Nuernberg trials around which film was made. Tracy portrays a fictitious character in the movie, which is not an exact chronicle of 1947 trials.

Article in The Oregonian, *September 29, 1961, in reference to Spencer Tracy's role in the movie* Judgement at Nuremberg *in which his character was based on Justice Brand*

Although scriptwriter Abby Mann had made use of Brand's "voluminous files, transcripts and correspondence" in penning the movie's script, Brand refused an invitation to go to Hollywood and meet Spencer Tracy. Similarly, although he was asked to consult on the movie, Justice Brand did not believe he could "ethically appear to endorse [the movie] as a factually, documentary account of events as they actually took place."

According to Justice Brand, the movie presented "a symbolic case, with truth in the air, but many instances of dramatic license taken." The film's producer, Stanley Kramer, echoed Justice Brand's perspective, noting that the movie was not a documentary, but a work based on historical fact, with dramatic license taken to "juggle dates to some extent and to combine actual characters for better entertainment values."[204]

The concluding two paragraphs of the newspaper's article focused on Burt Lancaster's character in the movie, Ernst Janning, and Brand's observations concerning the real-life basis for that character:

> The character played by Lancaster, that of the defendant, is in actuality a combination of two men: Franz Schleghberger [sic], minister of justice, a position equal to that of supreme court chief justice, and Oswald Rothaug, judge of the special court at [Nuremberg] [.]... Brand said Schleghberger [sic] was a man of great reputation, who disliked Nazi brutality but 'went along.' Rothaug, however, was a 'scoundrel' who in Brand's view, doesn't deserve Schleghberger's [sic] reputation.[205]

James Tenney Brand died on February 28, 1964, while vacationing in Phoenix, Arizona. He was 78 years old.[206] In his uncompleted manuscript on his Nuremberg experience, Brand chose to style himself as a "country lawyer" despite being a Harvard-educated legal scholar who could trace his ancestry to two governors of the Massachusetts Bay Colony. Brand's decision to describe himself in those humble terms may have simply been a nod to the broad scope of his Marshfield law practice as both a trial and appellate advocate, or perhaps because he had represented all manner of clients, from the Marshfield municipality, to corporate entities, to defendants accused of crimes. In any event, many saw him in a far brighter light than his own self-assessment would allow. James Brand understood that as a lawyer, he had obligations not just to his clients, but to the Bar, his community, and society as a whole. Throughout his professional life, he honored those obligations, first in Marshfield through his civic engagement, later in his leadership of the Oregon State Bar, his 17 years on the Oregon Supreme Court, and finally his service to a world emerging from war as a presiding judge at the Nuremberg Trials. "Country lawyer" or not, James Tenney Brand's personal and professional achievements stand as testaments to a life worthy of a prominent place in Oregon history.

James and Irene Brand

Epilogue

In 1886, the soon-to-be United States Supreme Court Justice Oliver Wendell Holmes Jr. addressed Harvard undergraduates in a speech entitled "The Profession of the Law." In it, Holmes described the reward that can come to those daring to aspire to great thoughts:

> For I say to you in all sadness of conviction, that to think great thoughts you must be heroes as well as idealists. Only when you have worked alone—when you have felt around you a black gulf of solitude more isolating than that which surrounds the dying man, and in despair have trusted to your own unshaken will— then only will you have achieved. Thus only can you gain the secret isolated joy of the thinker, who knows that, a hundred years after he is dead and forgotten, *men who never heard of him will be moving to the measure of his thought*—subtle rapture of a postponed power, which the world knows not because it has no external trappings, but which to his prophetic vision is more real than that which commands an army.[207] *[Emphasis added.]*

The notion that "men who never heard of him will be moving to the measure of his thought" would later prove prophetic in the case of James Brand.

Oregon Supreme Court records show that Justice Brand likely heard his first Oregon Supreme Court case two weeks after taking his place on the bench. Less than a month after that, Brand authored the written opinion in that matter, *State ex rel. Weingart v. Kiessenbeck.*[208] The legal issue in *Weingart* had been whether a father ordered to pay child support in 1933 for his minor daughter until she turned 18, was nevertheless required to pay support until the girl turned 21 due to changes in the age of majority enacted by the Oregon Legislature in 1935.

Father asserted that the 1933 decree had given him a vested right or property interest in ceasing child support payments after his daughter reached the age of 18. The upshot of that, father continued, was that he was being deprived of property without due process of law by the application in his case of the 1935 changes to the age of majority. Brand's opinion recognized that "in general terms, a judgment is personal property, giving rise to vested rights which the legislature cannot, by retroactive law, either destroy or diminish in value[]," but nevertheless rejected father's argument. Writing for a unanimous court, Brand reasoned that in marriage dissolution cases, the trial court retains jurisdiction over the matter and can subsequently modify the judgment so long as there is a minor child involved. Brand, in other words, recognized that a marriage dissolution judgment involving a child does not become final until the child reaches the age of majority. Because the child at issue in *Weingart* had not reached the age of majority when the law changed, Justice Brand concluded, father had no vested right to end his support obligation when his daughter turned 18.

Sixty-one years later in a unanimous 2002 opinion by Justice Thomas Balmer (also an Oberlin College graduate), the Oregon Supreme Court decided *DeMendoza v. Huffman*.[209] In *DeMendoza*, the court considered whether a statute requiring that a plaintiff recovering punitive damages pay 60 percent of the punitive damage award to the state, constituted an unconstitutional taking in violation of the Oregon Constitution. In rejecting that constitutional claim, the court quoted from Justice Brand's opinion in *Weingart*, and applied similar reasoning to conclude that "there is no 'long recognized' private property interest in a punitive damages award before judgment, it always has been at most an expectation." Whether any member of the court was familiar with the story of Justice James Tenney Brand, the court had nevertheless found itself "moving to the measure of his thought." The Oregon Supreme Court has undoubtedly relied on Justice Brand's reasoning in other cases not mentioned here, and will likely do so again in the years to come.

Acknowledgements

When a representative of the Holocaust Museum in Washington, D.C., told me that Oregon Supreme Court Justice James Brand had presided over the Nuremberg war crimes prosecution of the Nazi judges, I wondered, "Why am I just learning about this?" Despite that curiosity years passed before I decided to learn more about Justice Brand. I had a vague recollection that as a young lawyer in Salem, Oregon, I had met a Salem lawyer named Thomas Brand, who also taught business law at Willamette University. At my request, my son Peter DeMuniz, an investigator, determined that indeed Thomas Brand was James Brand's son. Peter located a court probate proceeding for Thomas Brand and that eventually led to my introduction to Justice Brand's living grandchildren, Ellen Ireland, James Asmussen, and Chris Asmussen. Their enthusiasm for the project, the generosity of their time, their donation of original family photos, original photos of the Nuremberg proceedings, an extensive family tree, and their grandmother's letters home from Nuremberg, truly breathed life into the book. I am profoundly grateful to Ellen, James, and Chris.

Kevin Hylton was my brilliant long-time clerk during my years on the Oregon Supreme Court. Kevin also wrote many of the speeches that I was privileged to give all over the world, in particular, during my seven years as Oregon's chief justice. Once I had written what I considered a working draft, I turned to Kevin for an initial review of the draft. As I suspected, Kevin's edits, comments, questions, and suggested additions, made the draft substantially better.

Thank you to Susan Irwin, archivist at Willamette University, for her assistance and many courtesies during my many visits to the Hatfield

Library Archives to study Justice Brand's records and personal papers from the Nuremberg Justice Case trial.

I also want to thank Willamette University College of Law Dean Brian Gallini, for assigning one of the school's top students, Colby Lewis, to confirm, edit, and put into proper form, my more than 200 end notes. And, thank you Colby for your excellent work.

I realize how fortunate I am that Hellgate Press, led by Harley Patrick, has enthusiastically provided me with the opportunity to tell Justice Brand's compelling life story. I am truly thankful for Harley's sensitivity and guidance in shaping the manuscript.

My wife, Mary, has initially and finally read and reread, every draft of each of my books. It was no different this time. To Mary, it's a family thing. My writing endeavors put the family name in print, it must be done well. The depth of her love and support for more than fifty-two years exists beyond measurement.

About the Author

The Honorable Paul J. De Muniz was elected to the Oregon Supreme Court in 2000 and served as chief justice and administrative head of the Oregon Judicial Branch from January 2006 to May 2012. He retired from the court in December 2012. Between 1990 and 2000, he sat on the Oregon Court of Appeals and served as a presiding judge. Before ascending to the bench, De Muniz was in private practice for 13 years with the Salem, Ore., law firm of Garrett, Seideman, Hemann, Robertson and De Muniz P.C., where he specialized in complex criminal and civil litigation, and appeals. From 1975 to 1977, he was a deputy public defender for the State of Oregon.

In addition to his work within Oregon, he also was a member of the Conference of Chief Justices and was elected to its board of directors in 2008. He has served on the boards of the National Judicial College, the National Crime Victim Law Institute, and the Institute for The Advancement of the American Legal System.

In 2011 DeMuniz completed a three-year term as a member of the Harvard Kennedy School's Executive Session for State Court Leaders in the 21st Century. That same year, DeMuniz was inducted into the National Center for State Courts' Warren E. Burger Society in recognition of his commitment to improving the administration of justice within the states.

In 2013 DeMuniz founded a legal clinic dedicated to providing legal assistance to previously incarcerated individuals re-entering the Salem/Marion County community.

During his judicial career DeMuniz spoke frequently to both national and international audiences on the importance of maintaining independent state judiciaries, improving state court administration and the need for adequate state court funding. He has served as the 2009 Justice Robert H. Jackson Lecturer for the National Judicial College. In 2010, he addressed judicial leaders from 55 countries at the Asian Pacific Courts Conference in Singapore, on the importance of judicial branch strategic planning. Later that year, DeMuniz gave the 17th annual Justice William Brennan Lecture on State Courts and Social Justice at New York University Law School, discussing the need for reengineering state court operations. In 2013 DeMuniz addressed the National Academy of Sciences in Washington, D.C. on the subject of evaluating eyewitness identification evidence in court.

In addition to his many law review articles on the courts and the legal profession, DeMuniz authored *A Practical Guide to Oregon Criminal Procedure and Practice*, a reference book used by lawyers and judges throughout Oregon, and co-authored *American Judicial Power: The State Court Perspective*, a legal treatise emphasizing the importance of America's state courts.

In 2002 DeMuniz founded a rule-of-law partnership with judicial leaders in the Russian Far East, working with lawyers and judges in Russia to implement reforms within the Russian criminal justice system. His work in Russia inspired his first novel *The Debt: An American Lawyer Fights for Justice in Russia*.

DeMuniz's work has been recognized with a number of state and national awards, among them: the National Judicial College's *2009 Distinguished Service Award*, the National Association of Criminal Defense Lawyers' *Judicial Recognition Award*, the Oregon Area Jewish Committee's *2010 Judge Learned Hand Lifetime Achievement Award*, the Oregon Hispanic Bar Association's *Paul J. DeMuniz Professionalism Award*, the Edwin J. Peterson *Racial Reconciliation Award*, the Oregon Criminal Defense Lawyers' Association *Ken Morrow Lifetime Achievement Award*, the Marion County Bar's *Paul DeMuniz Professionalism Award*, the Oregon Classroom Law Project's *2011 Legal Citizen of the Year Award*, the Campaign For Equal Justice *2012 Public Access to Justice Award*, and the 2013 Oregon State Bar *Judicial Excellence Award*. In 2020 DeMuniz was honored by the Salem, Oregon Chamber of Commerce as Salem's 2020 First Citizen.

He was raised by his mother in Portland, Ore., and attended Portland's public schools. After finishing high school, he enlisted in the U.S. Air Force and served a one-year tour of duty in Vietnam. Following his discharge from military service, he received his bachelor of science degree from Portland State University in 1972 and his juris doctor from Willamette University College of Law in 1975. In 2012, Willamette University awarded DeMuniz the honorary degree of Doctor of Laws. In 2016, he was awarded an honorary Doctor of Humane Letters from Portland State University. DeMuniz and his wife, Mary, reside in Salem, Ore., and have three grown children and six grandchildren. He currently teaches at Willamette University College of Law as a Distinguished Jurist in Residence.

Notes

In 2001, Thomas Bradstreet Brand, Justice Brand's son, and a Salem, Oregon lawyer, donated all the documents that his father had preserved from the Nuremberg Justice Case to the Willamette University Mark O. Hatfield Library. That treasure trove of documents includes the complete published transcript of the trial and judgment. The Hatfield Library has not inventoried their Nuremberg material so that the citations to those material are mostly general references to the Willamette University Hatfield Library. The Nuremberg Trials Project located at The Harvard Law School Library is an open access initiative that has digitized the texts of the pertinent documents from all of the Nuremberg War Crimes trials. Spending hours in the Hatfield Library archive studying Justice Brand's original hand-written notes and working with the published volumes of the transcript was a joy I had not anticipated. Harvard's Nuremberg Trials Project made it much easier to locate important sections of the original published transcript of the trial and the judgment. Two law reviews articles, Brian R. Gallini, *Nuremberg Lives On: How Justice Jackson's International Experience Continues to Shape Domestic Criminal Procedure*, Loyola University Chicago Law Journal 46, no. 1 (Fall 2014) and Bruce R. Jacob, *Judges At Nuremberg: Stetson's Connection To The War Crimes Trials*, Stetson Law Review, 44, no. 3 (2015) were also invaluable in directing me to original source material.

Introduction

1   James Tenney Brand, undated hand written note, Justice Case, Published Judgement Volume, Archive Section, Willamette University Hatfield Library, Salem, Or.

Prologue: Judgment at Nuremberg

2   Variety Staff, "Judgment at Nuremberg Review," Dec. 31, 1960, https://variety.com/1960/film/reviews/judgment-at-nuremberg-1200419953/.

Chapter One: A Famous Father and Family Roots in Colonial America

3   Robert Samuel Fletcher, *A History of Oberlin College From its Foundation Through The Civil War*, (Arno Press, 1971).

4   Roland M. Bauman, *Constructing Black Education at Oberlin College: A Documentary History*, (Athens: Ohio University Press (2010).

5   James Brand, *Twenty-Six Years Pastor of the First Congregational Church*, Oberlin, ed. K.J. Goodrich, 3rd ed. (1900) (excerpts on file with author).

6   Id.

7   Id.

8   Chris Asmussen, email to author, December 4, 2021.

9   Francis Juliette Hosford, *A Living Stone: The Story of the First Church in Oberlin*.)

10   A.L. Shumway and C. DeW. Brower, *Oberliniana, A Jubilee Volume of Semi-Historical Anecdotes connected with the past and present of Oberlin College*, Cleveland, OH: Home Publishing, 1883).

11   James Brand, *The Beasts of Ephesus*, (Chicago: Advance Publishing 1892).

12   Brand Family Tree (copy on file with author).

Chapter Two: Life and Education in Oberlin, Ohio

13   Bruce R. Jacob, "Judges at Nuremberg: Stetson's Connection To The War Crimes Trials," Stetson Law Review 44, no. 3 (2015) 699 n.13.

14   Arthur F. Benson, "James Tenney Brand," Nov. 7, 1945, Arthur F. Benson's Original Supreme Court of Oregon Document Collection, Oregon Judicial Department History, State of Oregon Library.

15   Ibid.

Chapter Three: A Lawyer Returns to Oregon

16   John W. Whitty, *Coos County Bench, Bar, and Beyond*, (CreateSpace Independent Publishing Platform, 2016) 234-35.

17   Ibid.

18   Brand Family Tree (copy on file with author).

19   See e.g., Bernitt Et. Al. v. City of Marshfield, 89 Or 556 (1918) (action
      to enjoin city officials from improving and grading a street); Rusk v.
      Montgomery Et. Al., 80 Or 93 (1916) (personal injury action); Cathcart
      v. City of Marshfield Et. Al., 89 Or 401 (1918) (action to recover damages
      for property damage); State v. Milosevich, 119 Or 404 (1926) (defendant
      charged and convicted of gambling); Rasor Et. Al. v. West Coast Develop-
      ment Co. Et. Al., 98 Or 581 (1920) (action against individual stockholders
      to recover on corporate debt).

20   Benson, "James Tenney Brand."

21   "Brand Backs Constitution," *The Oregonian*, May 15, 1941

22   Ibid.

23   Ibid.

24   Ibid.

Chapter Four: Oregon Supreme Court Justice

25   Ore. Const. art. VII, § 3, (amended by 1974 and 1996).

26   Ore Laws 1931 ch. 607, 610.

27   Hal E. Hoss, compiler, Proposed Constitutional Amendments and
      Measures (with Arguments) to be Submitted to the Voters of Oregon
      at the General Election, Tuesday November 8, 1932 (Salem, Ore.:. State
      Printing Department, 1932).

28   Brand Named To High Court, *The Oregonian*, May 14, 1941, A1.

29   See Oregon State Archives, Governor's Record Guides, https://sos.oregon
      gov/archives/Pages/records/governors guides.aspx.

30   Miranda v. Arizona, 384 U.S. 436 (1966).

31   State v. Folkes, 174 Or 568 (1944)

32   Douglas Perry, "Oregon's Murdered War Bride' Case Riveted Nation in
      1943," *The Oregonian*. August 12, 2021

33   State v. Linn, 179 Or 499 (1946).

34   Ibid.; 513.

35   Justice Brand's other criminal cases included a variety of matters. Justice
      Brand authored his first criminal opinion, in S*tate v. Wallace*, 179 Or 60
      (1942). In that case, the defendant had been charged and convicted of
      murder. On appeal, he argued that although he had failed to file a pretrial
      notice of his insanity defense and under Oregon law at that time had
      the burden to prove insanity, the trial court should have nevertheless
      instructed the jury regarding the elements of that defense. Brand's opinion

examined the issue from seemingly every angle that could provide the
defendant with a new trial. However, after examining every possible argument for reversal, Brand and the court affirmed the defendant's murder
conviction. Brand would later write an exhaustive article on the insanity
defense. In *State v. Nortin*, 170 Or 296 (1943) the defendant was accused of
murdering his mother but a jury found him guilty of the lesser-included
charge of manslaughter. On appeal, the defendant argued that because
there had been insufficient evidence supporting the murder charge, the
jury should not have been instructed on the lesser manslaughter charge.
Justice Brand wrote for a unanimous court and affirmed the defendant's
conviction for involuntary manslaughter. In doing so, Brand rejected the
defendant's insufficiency of evidence argument, an argument regarding
the admissibility of statements made by the defendant's wife regarding
the homicide, and an argument concerning the trial court's failure to give
an instruction on circumstantial evidence. In *State v. Dennis*, 177 Or 73
(1945), the defendant had been convicted of murdering his mother-in-law.
Because there was no direct evidence linking the defendant to the murder,
one of the issues on appeal was whether sufficient circumstantial evidence
existed to permit the jury to find the defendant guilty beyond a reasonable
doubt. In holding that the circumstantial evidence was indeed sufficient
to establish guilt, Justice Brand concluded the opinion by observing:
"With the utmost care we have examined 745 pages of testimony, 250
pages of defendant's brief, and more than 240 cases cited therein. We find
no reversible error." In *State v. Anthony*, 179 Or 282 (1946), the defendant
was found guilty of inserting a blunt instrument into the victim's anus
and through the rectal portion of her bowel and vagina with the intent
to commit an act of sexual perversion on the victim. The issue before the
court was whether the described act fell within the "catch-all" provision of
the statute outlawing "any act or practice of sexual perversity." After care-
fully analyzing the statute and concluding that the act fell within its reach,
Justice Brand wrote: "But we think the sex organ was as directly involved
as if penetration had been accomplished in a less brutal manner. As
performed the act brought the defendant not only to the door of the penitentiary but to the threshold of the execution chamber. It was only good
fortune that his victim did not die. The jury was warranted in inferring
from the evidence that the obscene act was performed for the purpose of
abnormal sexual satisfaction." In *State v. Opie*, 179 Or 187 (1946), the defendant was convicted of stealing a calf. On appeal, the defendant argued that
the text of the criminal statute under which he had been charged was so
indefinite that the statute reached conduct that was not criminal. Again,
the court's opinion was assigned to Justice Brand. In rejecting what Brand

described as a "void for vagueness" challenge to the statute, he quoted his own words from *State v. Anthony*, "But the rule of strict construction, if applicable, has little bearing in a case of this kind. The problem here is not whether we can extend a penal statute beyond the meaning of the words used. The question is whether we can properly limit the meaning of general words to cases reasonably within them and within the evil which the legislature intended to suppress."

Chapter Five: The First Nuremberg Tribunal

36   Arthur Krock, *End Comes Suddenly at Warm Springs*, N.Y. Times, April 13, 1945.

37   Telford Taylor, *The Anatomy of The Nuremberg Trials* (London: Bloomsbury, 1993) 22-26.

38   Norbert Ehrenfreund, *The Nuremberg Legacy: How the Nazi War Crimes Trial Changed the Course of History*, (New York: Palgrave, 2007), 7-8.

39   Robert H. Jackson, Address before The American Society of International Law, Washington, D.C., April 13, 1945, *American Society of International Law Proceeding* 39, no. 1 (1945): 15.

40   Justice Robert H. Jackson to President Harry S. Truman, memorandum, 29 April 1945, box 95, reel 1, Robert H. Jackson Papers, 1816-1983, Library of Congress, Washington, DC.

41   Ibid.

42   Robert H. Jackson, "Nuremberg in Retrospect: Legal Answer to International Lawlessness," *American Bar Association Journal* 35, no. 10 (October 1949): 814-16; Taylor, *The Anatomy of the Nuremberg Trials*, 59.

43   Ehrenfreund, *The Nuremberg Legacy*, 13.

44   Telford Taylor, *Final Report to the Secretary of the Army on the Nuernberg War Crimes Trials Under Control Council Law No. 10* (Washington, D.C.: U.S. G.P.O, 1949).

45   Charter of the International Military Tribunal ("London Agreement"), August 8, 1945, 82 U.N.T.S. 279. See also, Drexel A. Sprecher, *Inside the Nuremberg Trial: A Prosecutor's Comprehensive Account* (Lanham, Md.: University Press of America, 1999).

46   Robert H. Jackson, "Justice Jackson's Report to President Truman on the Legal Basis for Trial of War Criminals," Temple Law Quarterly 19, no. 3 (January 1946) 144-156.

47   Taylor, *Final Report*, 95.

48   Ibid. at 89-90.

49   Ley committed suicide on October 25, 1945 while awaiting trial. The charges against Krupp von Bohlen were stayed because he was bedridden, senile, and considered unfit for trial.

50   Eichmann was captured by Israeli Mossad agents in Argentina in May 1960 and was tried and convicted in Israel of war crimes. He was executed there by hanging in 1962.

51   Goering was also sentenced to death by hanging. He committed suicide, however, by ingesting cyanide hours before his scheduled execution.

52   Jackson, "Nuremberg in Retrospect," 340.

53   James Tenney Brand, "Nazi Justice," (unpublished partial manuscript), 3. Copy on file with author.

Chapter Six: A Decision to Prosecute German Judicial Officers

54   Taylor *Final Report*, 6, 9, 159, 251.

55   James T. Brand, "Crimes Against Humanity and The Nuremberg Trials," *Oregon Law Review* 28, no. 2 (February 1949) 93-119.

56   Allied Control Authority, "Control Council Law No. 10: Punishments of Persons Guilty of War Crimes, Crimes Against Peace and Against Humanity" in *Enactments and Approved Papers of the Control Council and Coordinating Committee*, vol. 1 (Legal Division, Office of Military Government for Germany, 1945), 306-8.

57   Benjamin B. Ferencz, "Nurnberg Trial Procedure and the Rights of the Accused," *Journal of Criminal Law and Criminology* 39, no. 2 (1948-1949): 144-51; William F. Meinecke, Jr., "German Justice on Trial: The Justice Case," *Military Law Review* 229, no. 2 (2021): 173-90.

58   Ibid.

59   Taylor, *Final Report*, 11.

60   Ibid., 20, 251.

Chapter Seven: Recruiting American Judges to Judge the German Judges

61   Taylor, *Final Report*, 34.

62   Ibid., 35, 157 n 73.

63   Ibid., 118-119.

64   Jacob, "Judges At Nuremberg," 707.

65   Taylor, *Final Report*, 35.

Chapter Eight: The Brands Go to Nuremberg

66   Brand, "Nazi Justice."

67   Exec. Order No. 9827, 12 Fed. Reg. 1215 (February 22, 1947).

68   Taylor, *Final Report*, 35.

69   Ibid.

70   Oral history interview with Hattie Bratzel Kremen, by Susan C. Glen, SR 1248, Oregon Historical Society Research Library. Accessed at https://digital collections.ohs.org/sr-1248-oral-history-interview-with-hattiebratzel-kremen. (Hereinafter, "Bratzel Oral History Interview").

71   Ibid.

72   In the opening scene of the 1961 movie, *Judgment at Nuremberg*, Spencer Tracy as Judge Dan Haywood is being driven through a war ravaged Nuremberg in a beat up army staff car with one star and a GI driver.

73   Irene Brand Letters to Family from Nuremberg, typed copies on file with author. (Hereinafter, "Irene Brand Letters,").

74   Ibid.

75   Ibid.

76   Ibid.

77   Ibid.

78   Ibid.

79   Ibid.

80   Robert Daniel Murphy had been appointed to serve as political advisor to Eisenhower to aid in the American occupation of Germany. As part of his appointment, Murphy had been granted the U.S. foreign service rank of Ambassador. "See U.S. At War: Ambassador to Germany?" *Time Magazine*, September 11, 1944.

81   Ibid.

Chapter Nine: Selecting and Charging the German Judicial Officials

82   Meinecke, "German Justice on Trial," 175.

83   Ibid.

84   Taylor, *Final Report*, 85.

85   Records of the United States Neurnberg War Crimes Trials, "United States of America v. Josef Altstötter et al. (Case III)," National Archives Microfilm Publication M889. (Hereinafter, "Altstötter Trial Transcript").

86   Ibid.

87   Ibid.

88   Ibid.

89   Ibid.

90   Ibid.

91   Ibid.

92   Ibid.

93   Ibid.

94   Ibid.

95   Ibid.

96   Ibid.

97   Ibid.

98   Ibid.

99   Ibid.

100 Ibid.

101 Ibid.

102 Ibid.

103 Ibid.

104 Ibid.

105 Ibid.

106 Ibid.

107 Ibid.

108 Ibid.

109 Ibid.

Chapter Ten: The German Defense Lawyers

110 Meinecke, "German Justice on Trial," 175.

111 Ferencz, "Nurnberg Trial Procedure," 146.

112 Ibid., 147.

113 Jamie McCord, "Justice, Nazis Got What they Never Gave," *The Oregonian Newspaper*, February 8, 1948.

114 "Altstötter Trial Transcript."

Chapter Eleven: Tribunal Number Three –
the Justice Case Trial

115 Brand, "Nazi Justice."

116 Irene Brand Letters.

117 "Altstötter Trial Transcript."

118 Ibid.

119 Ibid.

120 Ibid.; See Taylor, *Final Report*, 49.

121 "Altstötter Trial Transcript"; Brand's typed note on witness photo dated March 18, 1946. On file with the author.

122 Irene Brand Letters.

123 Ibid.

124 "Altstötter Trial Transcript"; Meinecke, "German Justice on Trial," 180-81.

125 "Altstötter Trial Transcript"; Meinecke, "German Justice on Trial," 181.

126 "Altstötter Trial Transcript"; Meinecke, "German Justice on Trial," 184-87.

127 Ibid.

128 "Altstötter Trial Transcript"; Irene Brand Letters.

129 "Altstötter Trial Transcript".

130 Brand, "Crimes Against Humanity and the Nürnberg Trials," 115. ("[T]he *ex post facto* rule condemns statutes which define as criminal acts committed before the statutes were passed.").

131 "Altstötter Trial Transcript."

132 Ibid.

Chapter Twelve: Judgment at Nuremberg

133 "Altstötter Trial Transcript."

134 "Altstötter Trial Transcript."

135 "Altstötter Trial Transcript."

136 "Altstötter Trial Transcript."

137 "Altstötter Trial Transcript."

138 "Altstötter Trial Transcript."

139 This appears to be a variation on William Shakespeare's Sonnet 116, a popular poem that included the couplet, "If this be error, and upon me proved, I never writ, nor no man ever loved." It is likely that Brand's

insertion of the Shakespeare Sonnet reflected Brand's life-long love of Shakespeare.

140 "Altstötter Trial Transcript."

141 Although 16 men were initially charged in the indictment, the tribunal only rendered verdicts on 14 of the defendants—the defendant Westphal committed suicide before the beginning of the trial, and the tribunal declared a mistrial as the defendant Engert due to his extreme illness during the trial.

142 "Altstötter Trial Transcript," 10,786-794.

143 Ibid. The Hague Conventions of 1899 and 1907 were a series of international treaties and declarations negotiated at two international peace conferences at The Hague in the Netherlands. The Hague conventions were among the first formal statements of the laws of war and war crimes in the body of secular international law. The Hague peace conferences of 1899 and 1907; a series of lectures delivered before the Johns Hopkins University in 1908. avalon.law.yale.edu.

144 Ibid.

145 Ibid.

146 Ibid.

147 Ibid.

148 Ibid., 10,794-821.

149 Ibid.

150 Ibid.

151 Ibid., 19,823-839. At some point during the trial, Rothenberger unsuccessfully attempted to kill himself by picking at his wrist arteries with a pin. According Brand, "Rothenberger was back to the trial in about a week, looking hardly the worse for wear but a bit sheepish." See also, McCord, "Justice."

152 "Altstötter Trial Transcript," 10,840-854.

153 Ibid.; 10,854-860.

154 Ibid.

155 Ibid.; 10,864-867.

156 Ibid.; 10,867-880.

157 Ibid.

158 Ibid.; 10,882-903.

159 Ibid.

160   Ibid.; 10,907-923.

161   Ibid.

162   Ibid.; 10,923-931.

163   Ibid.

164   Ibid.; 10,904-907.

165   Ibid.

166   Ibid.

167   Ibid.

168   Ibid.

169   Denazification in Germany was attempted through a series of directives issued by the Allied Control Council beginning in January 1946. "Denazification directives" identified specific people and groups and outlined judicial procedures and guidelines for handling them. Though all the occupying forces had agreed on the initiative, the methods used for denazification and the intensity with which they were applied differed between the occupation zones.

170   "Altstötter Trial Transcript," 10,904-907.

171   Ibid.; 10,932.

Chapter Thirteen: Sentencing the Justice Case Defendants

172   Ibid.

173   *United States Military Tribunal No. III Case No. 3*, [Nuremberg: Office of Military Government for Germany (US), 1947], PDF, https://digitalcommons.law.uga.edu/nmt3/6.

174   Ibid.

175   Ibid.

Chapter Fourteen: Returning to the Oregon Supreme Court

176   Irene Brand Letters.

177   Oregon Blue Book Earliest Authorities in Oregon-Supreme Court Justices of Oregon.

178   Bratzel Oral History Interview.

179   McCord, "Justice."

180   See Level v. Level, 183 Or 39 (1948) (domestic relations, child visitation); Starker v. Scott, 183 Or 10 (1948) (challenge to forest fire patrol

assessments and penalties); Stryker v. Level, 183 Or 59 (1948) (defamation); Dickerson v. Murfield, 183 Or 149 (1948) (property dispute); and Mackie v. McGraw, 183 Or 204 (1948). (personal injury).

181   State v. Long, 195 Or 81 (1952).

182   State v. Sack, 210 Or 552 (1956).

183   Arthur Weinberg, ed. *Attorney for the Damned: Clarence Darrow in the Courtroom* (Chicago: University Chicago Press, 1957).

184   State v. Hansen, 195 Or 169 (1952).

185   State v. Caputo, 202 Or 456 (1954).

186   State v. Cahill, 208 Or 538 (1956).

187   Or. Const. art. VII, § 3 provides, in part: "If the supreme court shall be of opinion, after consideration of all the matters thus submitted, that the judgment of the court appealed from was such as should have been rendered in the case, such judgment shall be affirmed, notwithstanding any error committed during the trial* * *."

188   "Justice Brand Calls for Reform, Sees Court Delay in Present System," *The Oregonian*, June 8, 1958, 1, 17.

189   Ibid.

Chapter Fifteen: The Final Years

190   Alpheus T. Mason, Harlan Fiske Stone: Pillar of the Law (New York: Viking, 1956), 716.

191   Ibid.

192   Hal Foust, "Prosecutor, Judge Clash Over War Trial," *The Oregonian*, Feb 23, 1948, 2.

193   Brand's speech to the American Bar Association in response to Wenne-rstrum's criticism of the Nuremberg proceedings is contained in Dean Jacob's law review article with a citation to *War Crimes Trials Upheld in Bar Talk*, newspaper article, date unknown (copy on file with Author). In addition, Dean Jacob points out that in another newspaper article, Brand countered Wennerstrum by arguing that persons violating the laws and customs of war have been tried by military commissions or court martial proceedings constituted by the victor for many years throughout the civilized world. "Brand Raps Judge's Attack on War Trials as Disservice," *The Oregonian*, Feb. 24, 1948, at 4.

194   Brand, "Crimes Against Humanity and the Nürnberg Trials," 93-119.

195   Ibid, 99.

196 Ibid, 115.

197 Ibid, 116.

198 In the extensive materials donated by Brand's son Thomas to the Willamette University Hatfield Library, is an uncompleted manuscript written by Thomas containing the same themes as his father's uncompleted
manuscript.

199 Brand, "Nazi Justice."

200 Jacob, "Judges at Nuremberg."

201 Ibid.

202 Phyllis Lauritz, "Nuernberg Trial Role of Oregonian Filmed," *The Oregonian*, Sept. 20, 1961.

203 Ibid.

204 Ibid.

205 Ibid.

206 "James T. Brand, Ex-Justice Dies," *The Statesman* (Salem, Or.), February
29, 1964, 1.

Epilogue

207 Mark DeWolfe Howe, compiler, *The Occasional Speeches of Justice Oliver
Wendell Holmes* (Cambridge, Mass.: Belknap Press, 1962), 28.

208 State ex rel. Weingart v. Kiessenbeck, 167 Or 25 (1941).

209 DeMendoza v. Huffman, 334 Or 425 (2002).

www.hellgatepress.com

www.ingramcontent.com/pod-product-compliance
Lightning Source LLC
Chambersburg PA
CBHW041922160426
42812CB00109B/3351/J